P9-DCL-128

This is the most talked about book on the Blackjack scene. This book has sold more copies in the past nine years than any other gaming book.

Prior to this new edition there was no possible way to learn how to play Blackjack accurately.

This is the only Blackjack book that is easy to understand and completely accurate, written for the beginner or for the expert player.

This is the first book written by someone who has been a successful professional Blackjack player. The author has spent more time playing Blackjack, more time in the casinos, and more time in research, than all of the others combined who have written Blackjack books or devised Blackjack systems.

The book features a' new Basic Strategy for one deck; the first accurate Strategy to be published for four decks; four easy to learn Count Strategies including the Revere Point Count Strategy which is the most accurate and most powerful strategy that has ever been published.

The strategies were devised from computer runs by Julian H. Braun of IBM Corporation who is recognized as the most capable man in the world in this field.

The book also exposes in detail many of the other Blackjack systems sold by mail order. 178 pages.

Playing Blackjack

as a Business

New Revised Edition

There is no fiction in this book. Everything is true. Every figure in the book is absolutely accurate. You will be shown how to play, and exactly why you make each play.

Playing Blackjack

as a Business

by

Lawrence Revere

A PROFESSIONAL PLAYER'S
APPROACH TO THE GAME OF "21"

The first book written about Blackjack
that is easy to understand and absolutely accurate.

A Lyle Stuart Book
Published by Carol Publishing Group

Carol Publishing Group Edition - 1993

Copyright © 1969 by Lawrence Revere
Revised 1971, 1973, 1975, 1977, 1980.
All rights reserved. No part of this book may be reproduced in any form, except by a newspaper or magazine reviewer who wishes to quote brief passages in connection with a review.

A Lyle Stuart Book
Published by Carol Publishing Group
Lyle Stuart is a registered trademark of Carol Communications, Inc.
Editorial Offices: 600 Madison Avenue, New York, NY 10022
Sales & Distribution Offices: 120 Enterprise Avenue, Secaucus, NJ 07094
In Canada: Canadian Manda Group, P.O. Box 920, Station U, Toronto, Ontario, M8Z 5P9, Canada
Queries regarding rights and permissions should be addressed to:
Carol Publishing Group, 600 Madison Avenue, New York, NY 10022

Manufactured in the United States of America
ISBN 0-8184-0064-1

40   39   38   37   36   35   34   33   32   31

Carol Publishing Group books are available at special discounts for bulk purchases, for sales promotions, fund raising, or educational purposes. Special editions can also be created to specifications. For details contact: Special Sales Department, Carol Publishing Group, 120 Enterprise Ave., Secaucus, NJ 07094

ABOUT THE AUTHOR

Lawrence Revere is truly an expert on Blackjack. He has been in the gambling world for twenty-seven years as pit boss, dealer, owner, trouble shooter and professional Blackjack player. He began dealing Blackjack at the age of thirteen in the back of an Iowa barber shop, worked his way through the University of Nebraska majoring in mathematics, then went west where he has been involved with gambling since 1943, in Nevada, California, Arizona, Montana and on the gambling ship off California. This background makes him the first author of a Blackjack book who actually made a lucrative business playing the game from both sides of the table.

Revere is a man ultimately capable of presenting the insider's view of gambling, as opposed to others who have studied the business from the outside, then written books by applying credible theories. Here is the voice of authority, speaking about what he knows best.

In addition to his talent as a professional Blackjack player, he has four years experience teaching Blackjack. He has developed simple teaching methods which enable the player to easily understand the rules of the game. Furthermore, after his simple explanation, he includes charts which help the player practice properly. Only a man with a complete knowledge of the game and the best techniques for teaching the game could write the perfect book for Blackjack players.

A Word on the Construction and Format of this Book

This book contains 70 charts, 36 of which are in color. I have found from teaching "21" that color charts are of great value in learning various strategies. By using color in the charts, the player can more readily see, understand, and learn.

The strategies in this book were devised with high speed computers by Julian H. Braun of IBM Corporation. He has taken Professor Thorp's original "21" program and substantially refined it to much more accurately analyze any strategy. He has also developed the first program to precisely analyze mathematical expectations for any given situation in the game of "21."

Prior to this book there has been no possible way for anyone to learn how to play Blackjack accurately.

This is the first time that the *correct* Basic Strategy has been published for the rules now in effect. This is also the first time an accurate Basic Strategy for four decks has been published.

The Revere Point Count presented in this book is the most accurate and most powerful strategy that has ever been published.

It required more than 9,000,000,000 computer dealt hands by Julian Braun to devise the Revere Strategies.

CONTENTS

THE BASIC STRATEGY CHARTS

These charts were designed to show you in the most simple way possible just why you make every play in the Basic Strategy. To guess or play a hunch, will only add to the casino's advantage. If players could win by guessing, there would be no casinos in Nevada.

THE BASIC STRATEGY CHARTS

THE COUNT STRATEGY CHARTS

HOW TO GET THE MOST
OUT OF THIS BOOK

If you were to pay $5, $500, or $5,000 for a Blackjack book or a Blackjack system, it would not benefit you in any way unless you were willing to study and practice for the time necessary to master it.

To become a successful Blackjack player, you must first learn the Basic Strategy. Basic Strategy is the correct way to play each hand when you have no knowledge of the remaining cards. It will take the average person four hours to learn the Basic Strategy. If you plan to play at all you need to learn Basic Strategy. Basic Strategy will not give you an advantage, but when playing Basic Strategy the house will no longer have the percentage in its favor. You will have an even gamble.

After you have learned the Basic Strategy, if you wish to learn a simple count strategy that is easy and will give you a small advantage, learn the Revere Fives Strategy. This will take an additional four hours.

If you plan to become a serious player and if you want more of an advantage, learn the Revere Plus-Minus Strategy. After you have learned the Basic Strategy, you can learn the Plus-Minus Strategy in about eight hours.

After you have played the Revere Plus-Minus strategy for a few weeks, you can learn the Revere Ten Count or the Revere Point Count. Do not attempt to learn either of these advanced strategies until after you have learned and played the Plus-Minus Strategy.

IF YOU PLAN TO BE A SUCCESSFUL PROFESSIONAL BLACKJACK PLAYER LEARN IN THIS EXACT MANNER. STEP BY STEP.

1. Read all of the book. Skip the charts.

2. Learn the Basic Strategy. Practice with Chart B-6. Do nothing until you can answer these questions without even a slow down.

3. Read all of the book again. You will have missed many important points. Study the charts in the Basic Strategy Chapter. Every chart is there for a reason. Learn why you make every play. Understand the game.

4. Practice Basic Strategy with Chart B-9.

5. Learn the Plus-Minus Strategy. Practice the count with Chart F-3. Practice the playing strategy with Chart B-9.

INTRODUCTION

Blackjack is the only casino game an amateur can learn to play and at which he can definitely win. My purpose is to show you the strategies which will make a winner of you just as they made a winner of me. I am a professional gambler—my single purpose is to beat the house at one of its own games. If winning is your goal, this book is written for you.

Prior to playing Blackjack for a living, I worked in the gambling world as a dealer, pit boss and owner. During the past nine years I have made my living exclusively by playing count strategies in casinos all over the world.

Recently, I have spent much of my time teaching my count strategies to those interested in becoming winning Blackjack players.

I have spent more time playing Blackjack, more time in research, and more time in casinos than all of the others combined who have written books about Blackjack and Blackjack systems. I believe that I know more about a Blackjack game than anyone else in the world.

This is the first book about Blackjack which is easy to understand, completely accurate and revealing. The learning process is simple—made possible by thirty-four years in the gambling industry and six years as a teacher of winning Blackjack. I explain Blackjack in the simplest way possible. I guide the player step by step and explain how to play each hand, and why. I also include practice charts to obtain maximum results as quickly as possible.

Until 1961, it was not generally known how to overcome the house odds at Blackjack. Then Dr. Edward O. Thorp wrote the book, "Beat The Dealer." This book, which at one time was on the best seller list of Time magazine, included a basic strategy for properly playing Blackjack. This strategy was proven to be correct by many computer experts, including Jet Propulsion Laboratory, IBM Corporation, Sperry Rand, Aberdeen Proving Ground, Los Alamos and General Dynamics. If you are to become a winning Blackjack player you must believe this.

There have been a number of books written on the subject of Blackjack and innumerable "winning systems" advertised and sold by mail. Most of them are hogwash.

The Optimum Strategy in Blackjack, by Roger Baldwin and others, which was published in 1956, was the forerunner on the scientific use of Basic Strategy, and was further refined by Dr. Edward O. Thorp in *Beat the Dealer*. Dr. Thorp's book, as well as *The Casino Gamblers Guide* by Dr. Allan Wilson and *The Theory of Gambling and Statistical Logic* by Richard Epstein have been up to now the only authoritative and accurate works available. In my book I have further refined and simplified Basic Strategy by a method which will equip the player to play each hand properly without doubt and without hesitation.

The advantage of knowing how to play each hand correctly is of tremendous value to you as a player. Then, later, you will learn merely by keeping track of the cards and learning a few simple charts that an amateur can readily become a professional. Just by keeping track of the fives, for example, you sometimes have an advantage of 3.6% over the house.

Anyone who plays count strategies at Blackjack is called a "counter." The house is afraid of counters. I will show you as simply as possible how to play as I do so that the casinos will fear you too, if they recognize you as an expert strategy player. The object is to prevent them from doing so.

Perhaps you have a mental picture of a professional gambler, the riverboat stereotype, for example, or the Mafia-type image. You would not recognize me, however, because it is my purpose to be as inconspicuous as possible. I dress as the average customer dresses, and I move into the casino as quietly as I can. When I sit down at a Blackjack table I continue to avoid attracting attention in any manner. I purposely play foolishly sometimes to prevent being spotted as a counter, and I occasionally even go so far as to lose bets deliberately.

Nevertheless, after working and playing in the Nevada casinos for many years, I know nearly everyone who is working in the Nevada gambling business, and they know me. I have finally been barred from playing in all Nevada casinos.

I am cold blooded. I play to win. I always practice a few minutes at home before playing to get into a Blackjack playing frame of mind. I will only play under the best playing conditions, and then, for no more than one hour in a single club. I never sit down at a table with more than two other players, and they must be good players. Bad players tend to change everything; mainly they disturb your concentration. If playing conditions are not right, wait and play the next day.

Always play within your bankroll, using no more than a percentage of it as a playing stake. Betting scared money is bad gambling.

I use one other cardinal rule: I do not drink when I work. If you wish to enjoy drinks and play casually, fine, but you will lose or win as luck dictates. I drink well myself, and I can handle one drink or twenty. But drinking and playing is like a diamond cutter getting all boozed up and trying to cut a diamond. You will want to be at your very best in order to use the advantages shown to you in this book.

It is also important for you to realize that even though the casinos have to be more careful, they are nevertheless aware that because players have realized they can win there has been an enormous increase in Blackjack play. Moreover, casinos are not as afraid of counters now as they were in 1966, because they know that in the final analysis, too few players have studied hard enough, or have followed the rules of play well enough to constitute a real threat.

If a player will devote himself diligently to the instructions I offer, there is every reason to believe that the casinos' fears will be rekindled.

If you truly want to win at Blackjack, I will explain to you as simply as I know how, with the aid of invaluable charts compiled over years of intense study and experience, how you can definitely win, either as a pastime, or to make a living.

You will not be gambling when you have learned the advantages set forth in this book. You will be in business.

Chapter 1
THE GAME OF BLACKJACK

You can legally bet on Dominos in the State of Texas, on Jai-Alai in Florida, and on a state lottery in New Hampshire. In Nevada, the only state with casino-type gambling, the most popular game is Blackjack or 21, a game now being played all over the world.

The first question most people are concerned about is: can you find an honest game? Much has been written on this subject, and much of what has been written tends to sensationalize the belief that, in Nevada, you cannot play without being cheated.

I will say from experience that a small casino with one or two games is a bad risk; you are in danger of being cheated every time you play. But as far as the large Nevada casinos are concerned, I was cheated only once.

On that occasion, I was playing casually in a large downtown Las Vegas casino. I had a date, and I was drinking. I was simply having fun. I was not particularly watching the dealer, because I did not dream that I might be cheated in such a club.

As the dealer picked up the cards from the previous hand, I saw him "peek" at the top card on the deck. He then dealt four "seconds" and took the ace of clubs for himself. (In dealing a second, the dealer slides the top card back, then deals the next card, keeping the top card for himself.)

I did not say anything at the time. We had been playing with two other players at the table, and I did not want to cause any trouble. But I went to the pit boss and told him what had happened. He denied the incident and suggested that I come back in the morning and talk to the manager.

The next day I did go to the manager, who in turn called the owner. I was told that this particular dealer was not capable of cheating, that poor old Ed could barely deal. Well, I had lost four hundred dollars to poor old Ed, and I was unhappy. I did some checking. Ed had been caught in a small Northern Nevada town doing the same thing just a short while before. Even though I had caught him cheating, the casino kept him there where he continued to cheat other players. I did not play there anymore, but I did get reports from other players that they were cheated.

But that was the single instance of cheating in my personal experience with large casinos. And I have played in them all repeatedly and for more than a quarter of a century.

Cheating can take place in a club without the knowledge of the owners. A pit boss and only one dealer may be involved. The dealer can cheat some players, then have a friend come in and "win" the "extra" money. But large casinos have a lookout overhead, television cameras, and a trained security force to watch for cheating dealers, and to watch for players who are cheating.

I have been told by many count players that they have been cheated in large casinos, but I believe that there were other reasons for their losses. The average counter has practiced at home for months. Playing under those conditions, he has never lost. He could, in fact, even take time to correct his mistakes. So when he loses in actual play, his first thought is that he was cheated.

Many people who gamble and lose think they have been cheated. Recently I was fishing in Montana and met a local couple who had recently returned from Reno. They told me they had been cheated out of sixteen hundred dollars at Harolds Club. This is impossible. No one has ever been cheated at Harolds Club.

Word gets out whenever a casino is cheating or "Running Flat," and it is only a short time until the casino is closed by Nevada authorities.

I have read most of the books written pertaining to Blackjack. Prior to this book, there have been only three others written about the game that were accurate. They were *Beat the Dealer* by Dr. Edward O. Thorp; *The Casino Gamblers Guide* by Dr. Allan Wilson; and *The Theory of Gambling and Statistical Logic* by Richard Epstein. These were written by very talented men and the strategies in their books were obtained with the use of computers. Much of the computer work was done by Julian Braun of IBM Corporation. Mr. Braun is recognized as the most capable man in this field. All the other books I have read were so inaccurate, and so foolish, that it was a waste of time to bother reading them. One book in particular, *Scarne's Complete Guide to Gambling*, by John Scarne, is especially poor. On the front cover of the book, it identifies Scarne as "The World's Foremost Gambling Authority." This is nonsense—almost any 21 dealer in Nevada could give you better advice on how to play Blackjack. Scarne's advice includes: double down on ten when the dealer has an ace up (this would be especially sporting). As I point out in the Basic Strategy chapter this play would cost you 16 additional bets in each 100 times that you played this way. He tells you to never split 44, 66, or 99. (Splitting 44, 66, and 99 at the proper time is a big gain.) But, he tells you to split two tens when the dealer has a five or six up, a play that only an amateur would make. I would not play at a table with anyone who played this badly. He also says to stand on 16 when the dealer has an ace up. This is cute. You would win 17 bets in each 100 times that you played this way. As indicated in Chart B-17, if you were to double down on hard 12 (a play that only an idiot would make), it would be a better play than to stand on 16 when the dealer has an ace up.

Obviously, there is one correct way to play each hand and only one way to play each hand. This correct strategy has not only been determined by Thorp, Wilson, Epstein and myself, but by all of the important laboratories in the world. And they all agree that a player, playing Basic Strategy, has an advantage of about 0.12% on the first hand dealt from a single deck when playing on the Las Vegas Strip where they have optimum rules.

I will say that I cannot agree with some of the inferences created by the colorful anecdotes Dr. Thorp supplies in his book, *Beat the Dealer*, or with certain of his attitudes concerning gambling in general. Obviously, he views the scene through the eyes of an amateur turned gambler, and many of his attitudes smack of old word-of-mouth cliches long associated with an outsider's view of the industry.

To drive home his point about cheating, Dr. Thorp cites the book, *The Green Felt Jungle*, co-authored by Ed Reid and Ovid Demaris. This is a difficult work to substantiate for the simple reason that there is no sure way to prove that what the authors say is absolutely true in every instance. Without such substantiation, it cannot be regarded as fact. Yet Dr. Thorp uses the book's references as if they were. Moreover, to carry his premise further, he cites examples by Reid and Demaris to relate how casino mobsters in various altercations have blown each other apart or taken money off the top before reporting income for taxes. He then moves directly to this statement: "Now let me ask you again, are men of the Cosa Nostra, who bribe public officials, who steal money off the top, who help to finance their rackets (dope, prostitution, and smuggling) with their casino profits, who commit murder to settle their differences—are these men going to stop short at a little cheating at cards?"

This is not a scientific hypothesis. It is by inference alone, indicating that members of the Cosa Nostra are everywhere in legalized gambling in Nevada. It infers that because this is true, operators in general will cheat in the same fashion that Cosa Nostra members always cheat. It is like using the following:

The pigeon is a dirty bird.

Canaries are birds.

Therefore, canaries are dirty.

This is an argument that will not hold up to scientific scrutiny because it is an attempt to prove guilt merely by association.

Dr. Thorp is free, of course, to retain his attitude toward the Nevada gambling industry in general; he is free to draw his conclusions from the various incidents which he relates in his book. The reader is also free to draw *his* own conclusions.

But when Dr. Thorp is dealing directly with the scientific, or mathematical phases of using strategies in the game of Blackjack, he should be trusted and respected implicitly. Where he has used the calculations of Julian Braun of IBM Corporation, his effective application of the theory of mathematical probabilities, as it applies to the game of Blackjack, is unquestionably correct.

If there is any shortcoming to this scientific presentation by Dr. Thorp, it lies in the fact that, to many of his readers, practical application of the strategies offered in his book is often extremely difficult to understand and put into play. This is undoubtedly due to the fact that not all potential counters have the mathematical background possessed by Dr. Thorp. Even though I have a mathematical background myself, and I have further refined this background by years of participation in actual gambling on the professional level, I found that it required over a year to master and put into play his advanced point count strategy.

It is my belief that once the reader has made use of the information supplied in this book, he will be in a much better position to read or re-read Dr. Thorp's work in order to take advantage of the various refinements there as suits his personal judgment. It cannot be denied that Dr. Thorp's books, devoted in the main to detailing various count strategies refined by him, have had tremendous impact on the game of Blackjack. Because of his book, the Nevada casinos changed the playing rules in April, 1964. These changes forbade the player to split two aces, and he could only double down on eleven. The rule changes were very unpopular; they were only in effect a brief time, then the casinos went back to the old rules.

Dr. Thorp's book was also responsible for the casinos dealing two and four deck games; this was done in an attempt to eliminate card counters.

Dr. Thorp has done a great service to the Nevada casinos by showing players they could win at Blackjack. True, he has made many count players, but the publicity was of more benefit to the casinos than any harm done by the counters.

Chapter 2
THE RULES OF THE GAME

Your first step to winning Blackjack is to learn the rules and how each one affects the game. Las Vegas has the best rules for the player. You may double down on any two cards. Some clubs stand on soft seventeen (A-6). Some clubs will let you double down after you split a pair. These are all good rules for the player. In Northern Nevada you can only double down on ten or eleven, and you cannot double down after you have split a pair. Each casino has a set of rules which generally agree with those of the other clubs in the area.

Some clubs in Nevada use two or four decks. In most casinos elsewhere in the world, four and six decks are used. (Atlantic City now is almost exclusively a city of six-deck tables.) Whatever the number of decks, your play will be basically the same.

The object of the game is to beat the dealer. You try to get a hand that is better than the dealer has, without exceeding 21. If you draw and get a total of more than 21 you "go busted." You then turn your cards face up and the dealer takes your money.

The game is played at a table with a dealer and from one to seven players. The game begins when the player places his bet in the small betting circle or square in front of him.

The dealer shuffles the cards in a flat, stylized fashion demanded by all the clubs. When the shuffle has been completed, the cards are offered to a player to be cut. The dealer may do this by extending the cutting privilege from player to player on a rotation basis, or by arbitrary selection. It is the player's prerogative to decline to cut the cards if he so desires, on the basis of luck or instinct, and allow

19

another player to cut them. After the cards have been cut, the dealer places the top card face up on the bottom of the deck: this is known as "The Burn Card." The dealer then deals two cards to each player and two cards to himself. The dealer's top card is turned up and is called "The Up Card." His other card is called "The Hole Card." The player's cards are both dealt face down as a general rule. However, in some clubs in Las Vegas, Reno, and other parts of the world, they are dealt face up. This will not give the dealer any advantage, for he must always play his hand according to fixed rules.

The player looks at his two cards, his "hand." If he has the right combination, a "standing hand," he slips his cards under his bet "he stands." If he does not have a standing hand, then he will want one or more additional cards. If he wants an additional card, he scratches his original cards across the felt, signaling for a "hit." The dealer then deals the player as many additional cards as he wants, one at a time. When the player is satisfied that he has the proper hand, he slips his first original two cards under his bet, and he stands. In drawing extra cards, should his count exceed 21, he busts, in which case he turns his cards over and the dealer takes his bet.

You count your hand as follows: Any ten or face card counts ten. Aces count one or eleven. All of the other cards count the number on the face of the card.

A Blackjack is an ace with a ten or face card, and is only counted as a Blackjack if it is your first two cards dealt. (If you split a pair of aces or tens and end up with an ace-ten, this is not a Blackjack.) Should a player be dealt a Blackjack, he turns his cards face up immediately and the dealer will pay him off at odds of three to two. If the player and the dealer each get a Blackjack, it's a tie or a "push."

The rules of the game are rigid for the dealer, but not for the player. The dealer must hit 16 or less, and he must stand on 17 or more. On the Las Vegas Strip, in Puerto Rico and some clubs in England, the dealer stands on soft seventeen (A-6).

Most all beginning players have trouble counting a hand with an ace or aces in it because they have been told that it is a "Soft Hand," and they are confused. If a new player has an ace and a four, and you ask him what hand he has, he will usually answer "five or fifteen."

Here is the way to count a hand with an ace in it.

The player has Ace-four. His hand is Ace-four.

The player has Ace-two-ace. His hand is Ace-three.

The player has Ace-six-ace. His hand is Ace-seven.

The player has Ace-ace-three-four. His hand is Ace-eight.

The player has Ace-six-four. His hand is Ace-ten. 21.

The player has Ace-six-five. His hand is Ace-eleven. 12.

There is a reason for counting your hand this way. If you will look at Chart A-1, you will notice:

If you have A2 to A6, if you do not double down, you always hit.

If you have A7, you only hit when the dealer has 9 or 10.

If you have A8 or A9, You never hit.

There are additional variation bets. These include doubling down and splitting pairs. There is also the insurance bet.

Doubling down may be accomplished by turning up the original two cards, doubling your bet, and receiving one card from the dealer.

The split bet may be chosen by the player when the first two

STUDY

cards dealt to him are a pair. He may then turn them face up and bet the same wager on each hand he previously bet on the single hand. After he splits the pair and draws another card to the split card, he may then double down if he has the right hand to double or continue to draw until he has a satisfactory hand. Should he draw another of the split cards, he may split them again. The exception is two aces. When you split two aces, you only get one card on each ace.

Chapter 3

A PREVIEW OF THE STRATEGIES

Presented here are six master charts designed to illustrate accurately and clearly the method of playing each of the strategies.

The new player will see at a glance exactly how to play each hand. The Basic Strategy Chart will explain itself. The new player will see with a quick study how these charts simplify the methods of play for every given strategy. Each strategy will be dealt with at length in the succeeding chapters.

In each chart, the column of figures running across the top from left to right represents the dealer's up card. The column of figures at the left running from top to bottom represents the player's initially dealt cards. The squares represent the action for the player to make in every instance. You match your hand with the dealer's up card, the consequent square gives you the play. The succeeding chapters will explain exactly how to learn each strategy, step by step, using the various simplification charts.

In most of the casinos throughout the world the dealer stands on soft seventeen, and the player is not allowed to double down after he has split a pair. The strategies in this book were devised for these rules.

When you are playing where the dealer hits soft seventeen:

HIT A7 vs 9-10-Ace

CHART A-1. THE BASIC STRATEGY

This is a guide to the playing rules for the Basic Strategy. The Basic Strategy is the foundation for all other strategies. You must learn the Basic Strategy first. In the chapter devoted to this phase of playing, I will explain why you make every play in the Basic Strategy and what you will gain or lose with every play. I will also explain why you must learn the rules set forth in this chart, rules you will be using eighty per cent of the time in every method of play.

If you are playing with a single deck and the rules allow you to double down after you split a pair, you split in this manner:

22,33,66	•	2 THRU 7 UP
44	• •	4-5-6 UP
77	• •	2 THRU 8 UP
99 EXCEPT	•	A-7-10 UP
AA,88	•	ALWAYS

H   HIT   S   STAND   D   DOUBLE   P   SPLIT

CHART A-1. THE BASIC STRATEGY

	2	3	4	5	6	7	8	9	10	ACE
62	H	H	H	H	H	H	H	H	H	H
53	H	H	H	D	D	H	H	H	H	H
9	D	D	D	D	D	H	H	H	H	H
10	D	D	D	D	D	D	D	D	H	H
11	D	D	D	D	D	D	D	D	D	D
12	H	H	S	S	S	H	H	H	H	H
13	S	S	S	S	S	H	H	H	H	H
14	S	S	S	S	S	H	H	H	H	H
15	S	S	S	S	S	H	H	H	H	H
16	S	S	S	S	S	H	H	H	H	H
A2	H	H	D	D	D	H	H	H	H	H
A3	H	H	D	D	D	H	H	H	H	H
A4	H	H	D	D	D	H	H	H	H	H
A5	H	H	D	D	D	H	H	H	H	H
A6	D	D	D	D	D	H	H	H	H	H
A7	S	D	D	D	D	S	S	H	H	S
A8	S	S	S	S	D	S	S	S	S	S
A9	S	S	S	S	S	S	S	S	S	S
AA	P	P	P	P	P	P	P	P	P	P
22	H	P	P	P	P	P	H	H	H	H
33	H	H	P	P	P	P	H	H	H	H
44	H	H	H	D	D	H	H	H	H	H
66	P	P	P	P	P	H	H	H	H	H
77	P	P	P	P	P	P	H	H	S	H
88	P	P	P	P	P	P	P	P	P	P
99	P	P	P	P	P	S	P	P	S	S
XX	S	S	S	S	S	S	S	S	S	S

CHART A-2. BASIC STRATEGY FOR FOUR OR MORE DECKS

This is your Basic Strategy when you play with four decks. There are fourteen changes from the one deck Basic Strategy.

When you are playing with four decks and the rules allow you to double down after you have split a pair, you split in this manner:

22,33,77	.	2 THRU 7	UP
44	. .	5 OR 6	UP
66	. .	2 THRU 6	UP
99 EXCEPT	.	A-7-10	UP
AA,88	. .	ALWAYS	

H HIT   S STAND   D DOUBLE   P SPLIT

CHART A-2. BASIC STRATEGY FOR FOUR OR MORE DECKS

	2	3	4	5	6	7	8	9	10	ACE
8	H	H	H	H	H	H	H	H	H	H
9	H	D	D	D	D	H	H	H	H	H
10	D	D	D	D	D	D	D	D	H	H
11	D	D	D	D	D	D	D	D	D	H
12	H	H	S	S	S	H	H	H	H	H
13	S	S	S	S	S	H	H	H	H	H
14	S	S	S	S	S	H	H	H	H	H
15	S	S	S	S	S	H	H	H	H	H
16	S	S	S	S	S	H	H	H	H	H
A2	H	H	H	D	D	H	H	H	H	H
A3	H	H	H	D	D	H	H	H	H	H
A4	H	H	D	D	D	H	H	H	H	H
A5	H	H	D	D	D	H	H	H	H	H
A6	H	D	D	D	D	H	H	H	H	H
A7	S	D	D	D	D	S	S	H	H	H
A8	S	S	S	S	S	S	S	S	S	S
A9	S	S	S	S	S	S	S	S	S	S
AA	P	P	P	P	P	P	P	P	P	P
22	H	H	P	P	P	P	H	H	H	H
33	H	H	P	P	P	P	H	H	H	H
44	H	H	H	H	H	H	H	H	H	H
66	H	P	P	P	P	H	H	H	H	H
77	P	P	P	P	P	P	H	H	H	H
88	P	P	P	P	P	P	P	P	P	P
99	P	P	P	P	P	S	P	P	S	S
XX	S	S	S	S	S	S	S	S	S	S

CHART A-3. THE REVERE FIVE COUNT STRATEGY

This chart illustrates how to play when you know that there is a shortage of fives in the remaining cards. You will keep track of only the fives. When you know there is a shortage of fives in the remaining cards, then you will act according to the rules of this chart.

This strategy is included to acquaint you with a simple method of counting cards. It will give you a greater insight into the more advanced counting systems.

I suggest that the beginning player learn this strategy first. He should play it for a few weeks, just for discipline, and to learn that if you follow the playing rules you will definitely win. Also, learning this strategy will be a big advantage to you later on if you plan to learn one of the more advanced strategies.

CHART A-3. THE REVERE FIVE COUNT STRATEGY

	2	3	4	5	6	7	8	9	10	ACE
62	H	H	D	D	D	H	H	H	H	H
53	H	H	D	D	D	H	H	H	H	H
9	D	D	D	D	D	D	H	H	H	H
10	D	D	D	D	D	D	D	D	D	D
11	D	D	D	D	D	D	D	D	D	D
12	S	S	S	S	S	H	H	H	H	H
13	S	S	S	S	S	H	H	H	H	H
14	S	S	S	S	S	H	H	H	H	H
15	S	S	S	S	S	H	H	S	S	H
16	S	S	S	S	S	H	H	S	S	H
A2	H	D	D	D	D	H	H	H	H	H
A3	H	D	D	D	D	H	H	H	H	H
A4	H	D	D	D	D	H	H	H	H	H
A5	H	H	D	D	D	H	H	H	H	H
A6	D	D	D	D	D	D	H	H	H	H
A7	D	D	D	D	D	S	S	H	H	S
A8	S	D	D	D	D	S	S	S	S	S
A9	S	S	S	S	D	S	S	S	S	S
AA	P	P	P	P	P	P	P	P	P	P
22	P	P	P	P	P	P	H	H	H	H
33	P	P	P	P	P	P	H	H	H	H
44	H	H	D	D	D	H	H	H	H	H
66	P	P	P	P	P	H	H	H	H	H
77	P	P	P	P	P	P	P	H	S	H
88	P	P	P	P	P	P	P	P	P	P
99	P	P	P	P	P	S	P	P	S	S
XX	S	S	S	S	P	S	S	S	S	S

CHART A-4.   THE REVERE PLUS MINUS STRATEGY

This chart illustrates the rules for playing the Plus Minus Count. You will learn in this chapter a simple method of following the cards, counting small cards as plus counts, and large cards as minus counts, as they are removed from the deck. When this has been accomplished, the rules of this chart will be all that you will have to learn in order to become an effective counter. I recommend that if you plan to become an advanced strategy player, you learn this strategy. Then you should play it for about two weeks. By that time you will be aware of what can happen in a casino. You will have learned to keep a count, and how to follow the playing rules that I will suggest.

CHART A-4. THE REVERE PLUS MINUS STRATEGY

	2	3	4	5	6	7	8	9	10	ACE
62	H	H	H	H	H	H	H	H	H	H
53	H	H	H	D H	D H	H	H	H	H	H
9	D H	D H	D H	D	D	H	H	H	H	H
10	D	D	D	D	D	D	D H	D H	H	H
11	D	D	D	D	D	D	D	D	D H	D H
12	H	S H	S H	S H	S H	H	H	H	H	H
13	S H	S H	S H	S	S	H	H	H	H	H
14	S H	S	S	S	S	H	H	H	H	H
15	S	S	S	S	S	H	H	H	H	H
16	S	S	S	S	S	H	H	H	S H	H
A2	H	H	D H	D H	D	H	H	H	H	H
A3	H	H	D H	D	D	H	H	H	H	H
A4	H	D H	D H	D	D	H	H	H	H	H
A5	H	H	D H	D	D	H	H	H	H	H
A6	D H	D	D	D	D	H	H	H	H	H
A7	D S	D S	D	D	D	S	S	H	H	S H
A8	S	S	D S	D S	D S	S	S	S	S	S
A9	S	S	S	S	S	S	S	S	S	S
AA	P	P	P	P	P	P	P	P	P	P
22	H	P H	P H	P	P	P	H	H	H	H
33	H	H	P	P	P	P	H	H	H	H
44	H	H	H	D H	D H	H	H	H	H	H
66	P H	P H	P H	P	P	H	H	H	H	H
77	P	P	P	P	P	P	H	H	S H	H
88	P	P	P	P	P	P	P	P	P	P
99	P S	P S	P	P	P	S	P	P	S	S
XX	S	S	S	S	S	S	S	S	S	S

CHART A-5. THE REVERE TEN COUNT STRATEGY

This is the basic blueprint for playing the Revere Ten Count. The chapter reserved for this strategy will show you how to keep track of the cards simply by counting tens and others. You will count forward. Where the squares indicate hit, stand, double down, or split, that is your play at all times. The numbers in the squares reveal the code count; in the Revere Ten Count Chapter you will be given complete code charts for every situation to match the code counts of this master chart. This strategy is entirely different from any previous ten count. You do not count backwards, and you have no ratios to figure. This system can be learned easily. The ten count has been the most popular of all the strategies.

CHART A-5. THE REVERE TEN COUNT STRATEGY

	2	3	4	5	6	7	8	9	10	ACE
8	H	H	7	6	5	H	H	H	H	H
9	5	5	4	3	3	6	H	H	H	H
10	D	D	D	D	D	2	3	4	6	7
11	D	D	D	D	D	D	3	4	4	5
12	6	5	5	5	5	H	H	H	H	H
13	5	4	4	3	4	H	H	H	H	H
14	4	4	3	2	3	H	H	H	H	H
15	3	3	S	S	S	H	H	H	6	H
16	S	S	S	S	S	H	H	7	5	9
17	S	S	S	S	S	S	S	S	S	3
A2	H	7	5	4	4	H	H	H	H	H
A3	H	6	5	4	D	H	H	H	H	H
A4	H	6	5	3	D	H	H	H	H	H
A5	H	6	5	3	D	H	H	H	H	H
A6	5	4	D	D	D	H	H	H	H	H
A7	6	5	D	D	D	S	S	H	H	5
A8	S	7	7	6	6	S	S	S	S	S
A9	S	S	8	8	8	S	S	S	S	S
AA	P	P	P	P	P	P	3	3	3	4
22	H	5	4	3	3	P	H	H	H	H
33	H	6	4	P	P	P	H	H	H	H
44	H	H	7	6	5	H	H	H	H	H
66	6	5	4	3	P	H	H	H	H	H
77	P	P	P	P	P	P	H	H	5	H
88	P	P	P	P	P	P	P	P	7	P
99	4	4	4	3	3	7	P	P	S	S
XX	S	S	7	6	7	S	S	S	S	S

CHART A-6.   THE REVERE POINT COUNT STRATEGY

This chart illustrates the playing strategy for the Revere Point Count Strategy. You will learn in this chapter a simple, but extremely accurate method of keeping track of the cards, counting small cards as plus counts, and large cards as minus counts, as they are removed from the deck. After you have learned the count, the rules of this chart will be all you will have to learn in order to become an expert strategy player.

Where the squares indicate hit, stand, double, or split, that is your play at all times. The numbers in the squares indicate how to play according to the count. You stand, split, or double, if your count equals or exceeds the number in the square.

In the Revere Point Count Chapter everything will be explained clearly and in detail.

CHART A-6. THE REVERE POINT COUNT STRATEGY

	2	3	4	5	6	7	8	9	10	ACE
8	H	H	+6	+3	+3	H	H	H	H	H
9	+1	0	-2	-4	-5	+3	H	H	H	H
10	D	D	D	D	D	-6	-3	-1	+4	+3
11	D	D	D	D	D	D	-6	-4	-3	-1
12	+3	+2	0	-2	-1	H	H	H	H	H
13	0	-1	-3	-5	-4	H	H	H	H	H
14	-3	-4	-5	S	S	H	H	H	H	H
15	-6	S	S	S	S	H	H	H	+5	H
16	S	S	S	S	S	H	H	+7	0	H
A2	H	+5	+1	-3	-4	H	H	H	H	H
A3	H	+5	-1	-5	D	H	H	H	H	H
A4	H	+3	-2	D	D	H	H	H	H	H
A5	H	+3	-2	D	D	H	H	H	H	H
A6	0	-3	D	D	D	H	H	H	H	H
A7	+1	-1	D	D	D	S	S	H	H	-2
A8	S	+4	+2	+1	0	S	S	S	S	S
A9	S	S	+7	+5	+5	S	S	S	S	S
AA	P	P	P	P	P	P	P	P	P	P
22	H	+2	-2	P	P	P	H	H	H	H
33	H	+5	-5	P	P	P	H	H	H	H
66	+2	+1	-1	-4	-6	H	H	H	H	H
77	P	P	P	P	P	P	H	H	0	H
88	P	P	P	P	P	P	P	P	+5	P
99	0	-3	-4	-6	-5	+6	P	P	S	+4
XX	S	S	+5	+4	+4	S	S	S	S	S

Chapter 4
BEHIND THE TABLES

In almost any business, the supervisors must be qualified for their jobs. If it is the construction business, bosses must understand almost all phases of construction. In the business world, the supervisors must have experience, special training, and usually a college education.

This is not true in the gambling business. The supervisors (pit bosses) as a general rule know very little about a Blackjack game. But they have the owners convinced that they can spot a counter as soon as he starts to play. There are not two pit bosses in a hundred that would know if someone was a counter or a carpenter.

When gambling became popular in Nevada, almost all of the pit bosses came here from other areas where there had been gambling. Most of them came from Florida and the Midwest. Generally they were crude and uneducated, and it would be rare to see one who had a high school education.

In clubs where they had previously worked, there had been no state supervision as there is in Nevada. There, the customers had always been cheated. The supervisors did not have to learn anything about the games. No one ever won. All that they had to do was to stand in the pit and look important.

In the past twenty years, they have needed pit bosses in Nevada. The new pit bosses have been trained by the old ones. Since they knew very little about the games, they could not tell the new pit bosses what to watch for. Also, they did not want the new ones to learn too much or they would not have a job themselves. Many of the old pit bosses still do not believe that anyone can win at Blackjack by keeping track of cards.

The main duty of a pit boss is to protect the house from being cheated. He should know what the dealer is doing and also what the player is doing at all times. He should be able to watch a Blackjack game and if anything unusual happens, he is supposed to see it.

Example: A very good player is playing Blackjack, the player is winning, he never makes a bad play. He knows how to play and he plays every hand perfectly. Then you notice:

1. On the first hand dealt, dealer has a ten up, he splits two 2s.

2. Next deal, first hand, he has an eleven, dealer has a 6, he does not double.

3. Later he splits two sevens, when the dealer has a ten up.

4. First hand, he doubles on nine, dealer has an ace up.

Every play is correct. There was an exact reason why he made each play. *Any* capable pit boss *should* be able to give you the right answer but I doubt that there are two pit bosses in the state that could give you the right answer to all of the plays. I do not think there are six pit bosses in the state that can tell for sure if someone is keeping track of the cards, if the player has an accurate system.

Most pit bosses get their jobs because of who they know, and not because of what they know. There are few who even know how to play basic Blackjack. They have no idea what an unusual play looks like. They might notice something like a card being bent, if it resembled a dip chip.

In almost any casino in the state, if a light bulb needed changing, it would take three pit bosses to do the job. One would have to hold the light bulb, while the other two turned the ladder.

The average pit boss operates about like this: a player comes to a vacant table and bets $5. He gets two tens, the dealer gets two tens. The next hand he bets $200. The pit boss now becomes alert and tells the dealer, "break the deck." The dealer shuffles the cards and the player walks away. That night when the pit boss sees the manager, he tells him: "We had a counter in today but I saw him in time. I had the dealer shuffle up and he left." This nut thinks that he has finally seen a counter. What he has seen is a typical "High Roller," playing in a style often identified with Oriental gamblers. But he has the boss convinced that he is really sharp.

There have been many players who were insulted, and even barred from playing because a pit boss *thought* they were counters.

Pit bosses are also supposed to suffer whenever anyone is winning. I saw one pit boss in Reno become so over-emotional because a player was winning at craps, that he walked around the table and started to fight with the man.

When I first came to Las Vegas, I was amazed to see men working in the pits who knew nothing about the games. Most pit bosses are there to talk about their golf games or the girls. They are also there to terrify the new dealers, to insult the girl dealers and to bother the cocktail waitresses.

Most of the pit bosses are also superstitious. I remember a pit boss who worked at the Mapes Hotel in Reno. This idiot thought that unless a dealer stood in a certain way that it would influence the way that the dice rolled or the way the cards came out. He also thought that if he stood in a certain way that it would influence the way the games went. He would watch a game and if the house began to lose he began a somewhat mystical dance: first he'd stand on one foot to thwart one player, then he'd switch to the other foot when the magic seemed called for. For a brief while he cultivated a color mystique. If a player got lucky and won a few bets he'd dash home and put on a red tie, then return to see its effect. One night a player was especially lucky and this pit boss rushed out only to return with both a red tie and a crimson jacket. He did not think it amusing that people began to notice him standing there on one leg in that garish outfit. This man later went to work for the Nevada Tax Commission as an expert investigator.

If you are playing and you are winning, a pit boss is usually standing near the table glaring and making you feel as if you had stolen the money. They will change the cards, and I have even seen them kick the dealer because he was unlucky. The average pit boss thinks one dealer is more unlucky than another. Many dealers are fired just for being unlucky. Some bosses blame the stick man on the crap table because they think he is responsible for the table losing.

Mistakes are made by the players and by the dealers. There are rules that cover all mistakes. The pit bosses are there to adjust the mistakes, and explain the rules to the players, and to make a decision when a dispute over a hand arises. Many pit bosses will always give the player the worst of the decision. Only a few pit bosses will give the player the best of it. I was working on a special assignment a few years ago in a Lake Tahoe casino. They had pit bosses working who knew so little about the rules of the game they could not explain to the player what the procedure was when a mistake was made.

Even if a pit boss should read this, he would not be insulted, because each one thinks that he is brilliant, and that this article is being written about the other pit bosses, not about him.

No one can really know what goes on in the casinos unless he has played the games from both sides of the tables for a living. The players who make their livings playing from the outside are constantly learning and practicing something new.

The most common complaint I hear from players is the way they are mistreated in casinos. To ordinary players, Blackjack is a fun game. People do not mind losing money but they want to have some fun, and they do not like arrogant dealers and pit bosses. The casinos need a training program to teach the employees common courtesy. Las Vegas is much worse than Reno and Lake Tahoe. The attitude in Las Vegas seems to be: we get 40,000 new tourists every day; we will never see them again, so be nice to no one. Many of the clubs insist dealers be overbearing and never speak to customers. The bosses know this will cut down on tips to dealers, and the house will get the money instead. This is bad business. Blackjack players, especially women, will look for a friendly dealer. If they find one, they will play with him whenever they play. They will skip the unfriendly clubs.

The young dealers do not like the $1 and $2 bettors—this is not exciting. Also, there is no hope for big tips. As a general rule, if a dealer is standing at a vacant table and a player comes to the table and makes him work, if the player is betting $5 or less, the player will be shown that he is annoying the dealer and he would rather he played somewhere else. The pit bosses do not see these things; if a pit boss is near the table, the dealer will wait until he leaves to show his displeasure.

The dealers in the casinos do not have it so good. They work one day at a time. They never know if they will work tomorrow. One honest mistake or a personality conflict and they can be fired. Some of the casinos will not let the dealers pick up their tips from the table. In some clubs if a player makes a bet for the dealer and wins, the dealer is not allowed to say, "Was that for me?" Some casinos will not let the dealer thank the player for a tip. They want the dealers to be discourteous so they will make fewer tips. Many dealers have been fired for allegedly hustling tips when they were really only being nice to a customer.

Of course if you're counting cards, the kind of treatment the clubs dish out to everyone makes it especially enjoyable to relieve these unmannerly, ungracious bums of some of their money.

Here is a suggestion to the Las Vegas casinos: In any other business I know of, if a customer spends his money he is given something in return, something of value. When a casino customer spends his money he is given nothing. The least he should receive is common courtesy.

Chapter 5

THE STRATEGY OF BASIC PLAY

To most Blackjack players, Blackjack is a guessing game. Every hand that they get is a guess with them. Sometimes they will hit 15 when the dealer has a large card up, sometimes they will stand. Sometimes they will double down on eleven, sometimes they will not. The average player has never read a book about Blackjack and he has no idea how to play the hands correctly. The average player will just not hit 16 when the dealer has a large card up, but if you will notice he will almost always hit 12, 13, and 14 when the dealer has a small card up. Almost every time that he gets a pair, he will split them without even looking to see what the dealer has for an up card.

I did not, for many years, think that anyone could beat a Blackjack game. Then I began to notice certain winners. They were not counters, but I saw as I studied their actions that they played in a different way. The primary difference was that those who hit the most had the greatest success. I have since discovered why.

Years ago people either played at home or at games they could find elsewhere. In those games, the dealer always won a tie. There was no point in drawing to a hand under that rule. You stood whenever you had twelve or more, and you won if the dealer went busted.

Now a tie is ruled a tie in casino gambling. Consequently you should draw more. Instinctively, or through experience, the winners I had watched years ago had found this to be true.

Others have since studied the strategy of basic play, using the highly efficient techniques of a computer age to prove the validity of

43

using controlling rules. Baldwin's was the first to be published in 1956. There have been others since. As I indicated earlier, the one who has created the most impact on the Nevada Blackjack scene has been Dr. Edward O. Thorp, whose theories virtually revolutionized the thinking toward the game by showing people how to become strategy players.

As in the case of Dr. Thorp's analysis, of Baldwin's and others, a careful study of all possible card combinations will produce an inevitable method for playing each hand as it is revealed to the player —a basic playing pattern, based on absolute rules for hitting, standing, doubling down and splitting pairs. This is illustrated in the Basic Strategy Chart A-1.

A quick study of the Basic Strategy will reveal that most of the rules are normal. But there are two situations which will seem extremely unusual. You will find dealers quickly telling you that you have made a mistake when you make these plays.

1. YOU HIT A7 WHEN THE DEALER HAS A NINE OR TEN SHOWING. This is a big gain for the players, an absolute must. But sometimes you will draw a bad card. Then the dealer will say, "But you had 18."

2. YOU HAVE A BLACKJACK, THE DEALER HAS AN ACE UP, AND YOU DO NOT TAKE INSURANCE. If the dealer has a Blackjack, he will say, "But you should always insure a Blackjack, you can't lose."

To achieve success a player must learn the Basic Strategy. He must learn it so well that he can play it without even thinking.

Very simply, the purpose of this strategy is to learn how to play each hand the right way—percentage-wise. To guess, to play the hunch, is to add to the advantage of the house, for the reason that guessing or playing the hunch results in bad playing. It has been computed that normal playing gives the house an advantage of between 5 and 10%.

You must learn the Basic Strategy first, because even if you do learn one of the count strategies, you will continue to play the Basic Strategy 80% of the time.

By playing correctly, the player actually has an advantage of 0.15% when he is playing on the Las Vegas Strip with best rules. Other casinos have different rules which proportionately affect your advantage. By playing the Basic Strategy religiously — studying hard, practicing for hours — you're playing an even game, rather than one where the odds are definitely against you.

HOW TO LEARN THE BASIC STRATEGY

How then do you grasp these rules for basic play?

I have found that the most effective way is to make up practice charts with all of the possible hands that you may get on them. Then go over the charts time and again, until the rules become an automatic mental response. I suggest that you make a copy of Chart B-6, carry this with you and go down the line and answer each question without any hesitation or thought. After you have learned Chart B-6 perfectly, go to Chart B-8, and when you have learned this procedure, make a copy of Chart B-9. You will always use this chart if you intend to learn one of the count strategies. Remember, *never make a mistake and never guess. Any decision that you are not sure of, check the chart.*

CHART B-1. HOW TO LEARN THE BASIC STRATEGY

TO BECOME A SUCCESSFUL BLACKJACK PLAYER YOU MUST LEARN THE BASIC STRATEGY AND YOU MUST BELIEVE IN IT. I SUGGEST THAT YOU LEARN IN THIS MANNER

1. Read all of the material, look the charts over, study them.

2. Study chart B-2.

3. After you have generally learned Chart B-2, practice with Chart B-6. This is the important chart. Do nothing until you can answer the questions without any thought or hesitation. This will take the average person four hours. (This is hard work.)

4. When you have mastered Chart B-6, practice with Chart B-8. Practice until you can answer these questions without even thinking. You will always use this chart to practice with. Do not use playing cards. It is more fun, but if you were to practice for weeks, some of the hands would never come up. This is faster and you get all of the decisions.

5. Every day or so read all of the material again. Study the charts until you understand exactly why you make each play.

6. Do not attempt to learn any of the other strategies until you know the Basic Strategy perfectly.

Remember: Never guess. Any decision that you are not sure of, check the chart. This is an attitude that must be perfected. *You must learn the Basic Strategy first.*

CHART B-2. PRIMARY BASIC STRATEGY

You have 5-6-7	Always hit.
You have 6-2	Always hit.
You have 5-3	Double if dealer has 5 or 6. Otherwise hit.
You have 9	Double if dealer has 2 thru 6. Otherwise hit.
You have 10	Double if dealer has 2 thru 9. Otherwise hit.
You have 11	Always double down.
You have 12	Always hit unless dealer has 4-5-6, then stand.
You have 13-14-15-16	Stand if dealer has 2-3-4-5-6. Hit 7-8-9-X-A.
You have 17-18-19-20	Always stand.
You have A2-A3-A4-A5	Double if dealer has 4-5-6. Otherwise hit.
You have A6	Double if dealer has 2-3-4-5-6. Otherwise hit.
You have A7	Double if dealer has 3-4-5-6.
	Stand if dealer has A-2-7-8.
	Hit if dealer has 9 or 10.
You have A8	Double if dealer has 6. Otherwise stand.
You have A9	Always stand.
You have AA	Always split them.
You have 22	Spilt if dealer has 3 thru 7. Otherwise hit.
You have 33	Split if dealer has 4 thru 7. Otherwise hit.
You have 44	Double if dealer has 5 or 6. Otherwise hit.
You have 55	Double if dealer has 2 thru 9. Otherwise hit.
You have 66	Split if dealer has 2 thru 6. Otherwise hit.
You have 77	Split 2 thru 7. Hit 8-9-A. Stand 10.
You have 88	Always split them.
You have 99	Split unless dealer has A-7-X, then stand.
You have XX	Never Split. Always stand.

When you have 8-9-10-11 or A2 to A8	Think, may I double.
When you have 12-13-14-15-16	Think, may I stand.
When you have a pair	Think, may I split.

It is important that you get to thinking in this way for the other strategies.

This chart was sent to me by a beginner. Maybe it will help you.

Thanks   b   b

CHART B-3. HIT STAND

	2	3	4	5	6	7	8	9	10	ACE
12	H	H	S	S	S	H	H	H	H	H
13	S	S	S	S	S	H	H	H	H	H
14	S	S	S	S	S	H	H	H	H	H
15	S	S	S	S	S	H	H	H	H	H
16	S	S	S	S	S	H	H	H	H	H
A7	S	D	D	D	D	S	S	H	H	S
77	P	P	P	P	P	P	H	H	S	H

S STAND   D DOUBLE   H HIT   P SPLIT

CHART B-3. HIT STAND

This chart illustrates what you do in all hit-stand situations as indicated in the rules of Chart A-1. Your hand is represented by the left column running up and down. The dealer's up card is indicated by the top column running across. To know the situation you match your hand with the dealer's up card—the consequent square gives you the play. (Example: If you have 12 and the dealer has two, you hit.)

CHART B-4. SPLIT PAIRS

This chart illustrates what you do when splitting pairs. It is read in the same fashion as chart A-1 (Example: If you have two nines and the dealer has a nine, you split them.)

CHART B-5. DOUBLE DOWN

This chart illustrates what you do in all double down situations, and is read in the same fashion as chart A-1. (Example: If you have A-6 and the dealer has a three, you double down.)

CHART B-4. SPLIT PAIRS

	2	3	4	5	6	7	8	9	10	ACE
AA	P	P	P	P	P	P	P	P	P	P
22	H	P	P	P	P	P	H	H	H	H
33	H	H	P	P	P	P	H	H	H	H
44	H	H	H	D	D	H	H	H	H	H
66	P	P	P	P	P	H	H	H	H	H
77	P	P	P	P	P	P	H	H	S	H
88	P	P	P	P	P	P	P	P	P	P
99	P	P	P	P	P	S	P	P	S	S
XX	S	S	S	S	S	S	S	S	S	S

CHART B-5. DOUBLE DOWN

	2	3	4	5	6	7	8	9	10	ACE
44	H	H	H	D	D	H	H	H	H	H
53	H	H	H	D	D	H	H	H	H	H
9	D	D	D	D	D	H	H	H	H	H
10	D	D	D	D	D	D	D	D	H	H
11	D	D	D	D	D	D	D	D	D	D
A2	H	H	D	D	D	H	H	H	H	H
A3	H	H	D	D	D	H	H	H	H	H
A4	H	H	D	D	D	H	H	H	H	H
A5	H	H	D	D	D	H	H	H	H	H
A6	D	D	D	D	D	H	H	H	H	H
A7	S	D	D	D	D	S	S	H	H	S
A8	S	S	S	S	D	S	S	S	S	S

CHART B-6. HOW TO LEARN THE BASIC STRATEGY

	2	3	4	5	6	7	8	9	X	A
12	H	H	S	S	S	H	H	H	H	H
13	S	S	S	S	S	H	H	H	H	H
14	S	S	S	S	S	H	H	H	H	H
15	S	S	S	S	S	H	H	H	H	H
16	S	S	S	S	S	H	H	H	H	H

WHEN DEALER HAS A SMALL CARD

2 3 4 5 6

YOU NEVER HIT 13-14-15-16

HIT 12 IF DEALER HAS 2 OR 3

WHEN DEALER HAS A LARGE CARD

7 8 9 10 ACE

HIT UNTIL YOU GET 17

DOUBLE DOWN

DOUBLE ON 10	EXCEPT 10 OR ACE
DOUBLE ON 9	2 THRU 6
DOUBLE ON 8	5 OR 6 (NO 6-2)
DOUBLE A2-A5	4-5-6
DOUBLE ON A6	2 THRU 6
DOUBLE ON A7	3 THRU 6
DOUBLE ON A8	6 ONLY

SPLIT PAIRS

22	3 THRU 7
33	4 THRU 7
66	2 THRU 6
77	2 THRU 7
99	EXCEPT ACE-7-10

A2 TO A6

IF YOU CANT DOUBLE DOWN ALWAYS HIT

YOU HAVE A-7

A-2-7-8	STAND
3-4-5-6	DOUBLE
9 OR 10	HIT

A8 OR A9

IF YOU CANT DOUBLE DOWN ALWAYS STAND

WHEN DO YOU DO YOU DOUBLE ON 10
WHEN DO YOU HIT A-7
WHEN DO YOU DOUBLE ON A-2
WHEN DO YOU HIT 14
WHEN DO YOU SPLIT 2-2
WHEN DO YOU STAND ON A-6
WHEN DO YOU DOUBLE ON 8
WHEN DO YOU STAND ON 15
WHEN DO YOU SPLIT 4-4
WHEN DO YOU STAND ON A-5
WHEN DO YOU DOUBLE ON A-7
WHEN DO YOU HIT 16
WHEN DO YOU SPLIT 6-6
WHEN DO YOU HIT A-8
WHEN DO YOU DOUBLE ON A-4
WHEN DO YOU STAND ON 13
WHEN DO YOU SPLIT 8-8
WHEN DO YOU STAND ON A-6
WHEN DO YOU DOUBLE ON 11
WHEN DO YOU HIT 12
WHEN DO YOU SPLIT 3-3
WHEN DO YOU HIT A-5
WHEN DO YOU STAND ON 14
WHEN DO YOU DOUBLE ON A-5
WHEN DO YOU SPLIT 5-5
WHEN DO YOU STAND ON 9-9
WHEN DO YOU HIT 15
WHEN DO YOU DOUBLE ON 9
WHEN DO YOU SPLIT 7-7
WHEN DO YOU STAND ON A-7
WHEN DO YOU DOUBLE ON A-8
WHEN DO YOU STAND ON 12
WHEN DO YOU DOUBLE ON A-3
WHEN DO YOU HIT 13
WHEN DO YOU SPLIT 9-9
WHEN DO YOU STAND ON A-8
WHEN DO YOU DOUBLE ON A-6
WHEN DO YOU STAND ON 16
WHEN DO YOU DOUBLE ON A-9
WHEN DO YOU SPLIT A-A
WHEN DO YOU STAND ON 7-7

ASK YOURSELF THE QUESTIONS ABOVE THEN
CHECK THE ANSWERS TO THE LEFT. GO OVER
AND OVER THESE QUESTIONS. THIS IS THE
EASIEST WAY TO LEARN HOW TO PLAY.

EVERYTHING YOU SEE HERE IS ABSOLUTELY
CORRECT. YOU MUST BELIEVE THIS.

DO NOT ATTEMPT TO LEARN ANYTHING ELSE
UNTIL YOU CAN GO OVER THESE QUESTIONS
AND ANSWER THEM INSTANTLY. AFTER YOU
HAVE LEARNED THIS CHART PRACTICE WITH
CHART B-8. THEN WITH CHART B-9.

CHART B-7. BASIC BLACKJACK

<u>HIT--STAND</u>

```
4-5-6      UP   HIT TIL YOU GET 12
2 OR 3     UP   HIT TIL YOU GET 13
7-8-9-X-A UP    HIT TIL YOU GET 17
```

<u>DOUBLE DOWN</u>

```
DOUBLE ON  8      5 OR 6       UP   (NO 6-2)
DOUBLE ON  9      2 THRU 6     UP
DOUBLE ON 10      2 THRU 9     UP
DOUBLE ON 11      ALWAYS
DOUBLE A2-A5      4-5-6        UP
DOUBLE ON A6      2 THRU 6     UP
DOUBLE ON A7      3-4-5-6      UP
DOUBLE ON A8      6 ONLY
```

<u>SPLIT PAIRS</u>

```
22                3 THRU 7     UP
33                4 THRU 7     UP
66                2 THRU 6     UP
77                2 THRU 7     UP
99      EXCEPT    A-7-10       UP
AA,88             ALWAYS
```

<u>A2 TO A6</u>

```
IF YOU CANT DOUBLE  ALWAYS HIT
```

<u>YOU HAVE A7</u>

```
3-4-5-6  UP          DOUBLE
A-2-7-8  UP          STAND
9 OR 10  UP          HIT
```

<u>A8 OR A9</u>

```
IF YOU CANT DOUBLE ALWAYS STAND
```

CHART B-7.   BASIC BLACKJACK

This chart is the same as Chart A-1. It is in a different form that is easier to memorize. You should make a copy of this chart to use as a check for your memory, employing it to practice Chart B-8 and B-9. Carry this chart with you at all times, Study this chart over morning coffee, while shaving, while riding the bus, during TV commercials—at any time that you have a few minutes.

CHART B-8. PRACTICE HANDS

HIT STAND

15 9	15 A	16 9	15 5	14 X	14 6
13 5	13 6	14 7	14 8	16 6	13 X
16 8	16 2	16 X	16 A	14 5	16 3
12 4	12 5	12 6	12 2	12 3	16 7
15 2	15 8	15 X	15 7	13 A	14 9
16 5	14 5	13 3	13 4	13 2	14 6
A7 7	A7 A	A7 8	A7 X	A7 9	77 X

DOUBLE DOWN

10 4	10 5	10 6	10 7	10 8	10 9
9 7	9 8	9 3	9 4	9 5	9 2
A4 4	A4 3	A5 3	A4 5	A5 4	A5 5
11 9	11 X	11 A	11 2	11 3	11 4
A2 3	A2 5	A2 6	A3 3	A3 4	A3 6
A5 6	A6 6	A6 3	A6 4	A6 5	A6 2
62 4	53 5	62 6	53 3	62 5	53 6
A7 3	A7 4	A7 5	A7 6	A8 3	A8 6
11 5	11 6	11 7	A2 4	A3 5	A4 6

SPLIT PAIRS

99 4	99 5	99 6	99 7	99 8	99 9
44 2	44 3	44 4	44 5	44 6	88 X
77 6	77 7	77 8	77 2	77 3	77 9
66 4	66 5	66 6	66 7	66 2	66 8
22 3	22 4	22 5	22 8	22 7	22 2
33 7	33 8	33 2	33 3	33 4	44 7
99 X	99 A	99 2	99 3	AA A	AA X

CHART B-8. PRACTICE HANDS

This chart contains all of the problem hands that can come up. Practice by going down each line, asking yourself the questions. Example: You have 15, the dealer has a 9 up, what do you do? If you are not sure of the answer, simply check it against the practice chart on the table beside you. The point of this entire practice is that you might deal hands for weeks, using a normal deck, and some hands will never show up. Also this is much faster. You will use this chart to learn any of the count strategies.

CHART B-9. ALL OF THE PROBLEM HANDS

12 6	53 4	53 6	53 5	A7 X	44 7	62 6
AA 3	12 2	12 4	16 2	12 3	13 2	12 5
14 2	A2 4	A4 3	A2 6	A4 5	A2 5	A2 3
10 9	73 3	64 X	55 2	82 4	73 8	64 5
44 6	AA 9	AA X	AA 2	AA 7	AA 8	AA A
13 8	13 6	15 5	13 3	13 5	14 6	14 4
A8 5	33 8	33 3	33 5	33 7	33 2	33 4
33 6	A6 2	A6 6	A4 4	A6 4	A6 5	A7 3
A7 2	44 4	62 5	44 3	44 2	88 9	44 5
13 4	16 5	14 3	14 5	15 2	15 4	15 6
A4 6	55 7	83 9	74 A	82 6	73 A	A4 2
65 7	22 4	22 6	22 8	22 5	22 3	22 7
22 2	A8 3	A3 5	A6 3	A8 2	A8 4	A8 6
15 3	66 6	66 7	88 X	66 3	66 5	66 2
66 4	63 4	54 8	72 3	63 5	54 2	72 7
72 6	16 8	15 7	14 8	14 7	15 8	A9 4
53 3	A3 3	A5 6	A5 5	A3 4	A3 6	16 7
A5 4	15 X	16 3	16 X	16 6	14 X	74 2
77 2	77 4	77 6	A7 A	77 8	77 3	77 5
99 5	83 X	13 A	15 9	16 A	16 9	A5 3
15 A	14 9	74 5	65 4	92 6	83 3	16 4
92 8	99 7	99 A	99 2	99 4	99 6	99 3
A9 5	A7 6	A9 3	A7 4	A9 6	A7 5	14 A

CHART B-9. ALL OF THE PROBLEM HANDS

All of the possible problem hands that you can get are on this Chart. *After* you have learned Chart B-6 perfectly, so that you can answer each question instantly, and you can answer the questions in Chart B-8, *then* use this chart to practice with. Start at the top left corner, go down the line, ask yourself each question. If you are not sure of the answer, *do not guess,* look for the answer on Chart A-1. Get into the habit of never guessing, be sure of everything you do. You will use this Chart to practice any of the count strategies. You must learn this chart perfectly.

CHART B-10. PLAYER'S GAIN BY DRAWING

This chart illustrates the player's gain by drawing, as against standing, with hard totals. The left column running up and down represents the player's hand. The column running across represents the dealer's up card. The squares represent the results of drawing, instead of standing. The plus figures indicate the number of bets a player will gain in each 100 draws. The minus figures indicate the number of bets a player will lose in each 100 draws. (Example: If the player's hand is 12 and he draws to it when the dealer shows a 2, he will gain 4 bets in each 100 draws. If the player's hand is 13 and the dealer has a 2 up, if the player draws he will lose 2 additional bets in each 100 draws.)

By checking these results against Chart A-1 you can see why the rules for play have been created. You see now that there is a definite way to play each hand. If it is a gain to hit 12 when the dealer has a 2 up, then this you must do. In the Basic Strategy, and in all of the count strategies, you must do exactly as the chart says. It is the correct way to play.

CHART B-10. PLAYERS GAIN BY DRAWING — HARD TOTALS

	2	3	4	5	6	7	8	9	TEN	ACE
12	4	1	- 2	- 5	- 2	21	19	14	16	25
13	- 2	- 4	- 9	-12	- 9	17	15	14	12	22
14	- 8	-12	-16	-19	-17	11	14	10	7	19
15	-14	-18	-22	-26	-23	12	11	6	4	16
16	-17	-21	-26	-30	-26	11	10	5	3	15
17	-38	-42	-47	-45	-47	-33	- 8	-11	-15	- 9

PLAYERS GAIN BY DRAWING — SOFT TOTALS

	2	3	4	5	6	7	8·	9	TEN	ACE
A6	14	13	12	14	13	15	32	27	23	29
A7	- 7	- 7	- 5	- 5	- 7	-23	- 7	9	4	0
A8	-28	-25	-23	-24	-24	-39	-44	-28	-16	-30
A9	-47	-45	-43	-42	-42	-53	-61	-66	-55	-61

A certain psychological attitude must be achieved. You *must* trust absolutely in the system, and you *must* do exactly as the rules state. *If the chart says hit, you must always hit without any ideas of your own.* In the beginning it will be hard not to guess. It was for me. (Example: You have a 16, the dealer has a seven. You just know that if you draw you are going to bust. You have to learn never to think like this. You have to think, "If I stand on 16 when the dealer has a 7 up, I will only win one bet in four." So you hit.) You will not be right all of the time, just most of the time. But this is the attitude you must perfect.

I am not a psychologist—and certainly not one of the female sex, but I know from experience that most pit bosses believe that all female players are stupid. It seems that every hand is a guess with women. They just will not believe that there is an exact way to play every hand. Because this book is being written for women as well as men, a challenge is hereby offered: *If a woman learns to play as expertly as this book can teach her, she can win a million dollars simply with the advantage of being female.*

I recall a personal experience when I spent weeks teaching a girl to play. I explained everything to her, including all of the finer points, such as why you hit until you get 17 when the dealer has a large card up; why you stand on 13 to 16 when the dealer has a small card up; why, in short, it is very important never to guess, because everything in the Basic Strategy is the correct thing to do. This Basic Strategy has been proven on a computer, not by one person, but by many.

Finally, we went out to play.

On the very first hand she got 15. The dealer had a seven. She thought for awhile, finally she stood. In astonishment I asked her why. She said, "I had a hunch."

There was, perhaps, something of the feminine mystique involved. Women are reputed to have that extra instinct. It is possible they are more inclined to rely on hunch. But *the attitude of depending totally on the rules for basic strategy is the only attitude possible for winning in the long run.*

You must know that when the dealer has a seven, he will make 17 or better 74 times in each 100 hands. If you stand short, you will win one bet in four—the times he goes busted. If you draw you will help 40% of the time.

As you continue on to the count strategies, you will notice that you may sometimes stand on 16 when the dealer has a ten, but you will hit 16 if he has a 7. When I first started playing this seemed unusual. When the dealer has a ten, he quite likely has 20 or a bad hand. If you draw to 16, there is only one card that you can draw and beat 20, you must draw a 5. When the dealer has 7 and you draw, if you catch an ace, 2, 3, 4, or 5, you have accomplished something big and you probably have a winning hand. Hitting 16 when the dealer has a ten is a very close play, as you will learn later, and you will generally stand if you have any three card 16 and the dealer has a ten up.

Most of the other books that have been written on Blackjack were written for the experienced player. They give very little consideration to the beginner.

As I have mentioned before, my intention when I started writing this book was to make everything as simple as possible. Some of the material may seem too simple. But from teaching beginners, I have learned that you must paint them a clear picture of everything. As an example: In my first basic strategy, I had: You double down on 5-3 if the dealer has a five or six up. Then some students would ask: "What do you mean, up. How far up?" I corrected that by omitting the word up. Another student asked, "If you double down on 5-3 when the dealer has a five or six, what do you do when he has a nine?" You would think that they could figure out something as simple as that.

CHART B-11. WHY YOU MAKE CERTAIN PLAYS

Why are these situations absolute? In terms of each 100 hands played, Chart B-11 illustrates what happens in three different situations. It also explains a very important point in Basic Strategy concerning the insuring of a Blackjack. My point in including this chart is to illustrate exactly why these situations produce their effects.

CHART B-11. WHY YOU MAKE CERTAIN PLAYS

YOU HAVE 16 THE DEALER HAS A 7 UP

YOU HAVE A LOUSY HAND, THE WORST HAND YOU COULD GET. YOU FIGURE TO LOSE.
DEALER WILL BREAK 26 TIMES IN 100. IF YOU STAND YOU WILL WIN 26 BETS.

IF YOU DRAW 100 TIMES YOU WILL MAKE:

8	21s
8	20s
8	19s
8	18s
8	17s

IF YOU STAND YOU LOSE 48 UNITS IN EACH 100 HANDS. IF YOU DRAW YOU ONLY
LOSE 37 UNITS IN EACH 100 HANDS. YOU GAIN 11 UNITS IN EACH 100 DRAWS.

SO, WHEN THE DEALER HAS 7-8-9-10-ACE UP, YOU MUST HIT UNTIL YOU GET 17.

YOU HAVE A-7 THE DEALER HAS A 9 OR 10 UP

YOU HAVE A LOSING HAND. WHEN THE DEALER HAS A NINE OR TEN UP HIS AVERAGE
HAND WILL BE 19 OR MORE. YOU MUST HIT. EVEN IF YOU DRAW A FOUR YOU HAVE
ALMOST THE SAME HAND. BY DRAWING YOU WILL GAIN 7 BETS IN EACH 100 HANDS.

YOU HAVE 8-8 THE DEALER HAS A 10 UP

YOU HAVE ANOTHER POOR HAND AND FIGURE TO LOSE. SPLIT THEM YOU WILL MAKE:

14	21s	73	18s
14	20s	26	17s
29	19s		

IF YOU STAND YOU WILL WIN 23 BETS. IF YOU DRAW YOU WILL WIN 26 BETS. IF
YOU SPLIT THEM YOU WILL GAIN 6 BETS IN EACH 100 SPLITS.

ANYTIME YOU GET TWO EIGHTS YOU MUST SPLIT THEM, IT IS ALWAYS A BIG GAIN
AGAINST ANY UP CARD.

DO NOT INSURE A BLACKJACK

IF YOU HOLD A BLACKJACK YOURSELF INSURANCE IS A BAD BET. DO NOT TAKE IT.
THE ODDS ARE 34-15 AGAINST A PAYOFF OF 30-15. YOU ARE GIVING THE HOUSE A
BIG FAT 8% WHEN YOU INSURE A BLACKJACK. YOU NEVER TAKE INSURANCE UNLESS
YOU ARE COUNTING CARDS.

CHART B-12. GAIN BY DOUBLING DOWN AND SPLITTING PAIRS

This chart illustrates the player's gain or loss when he doubles down or splits a pair. The left column running up and down represents the player's hand. The top column running across represents the dealer's up card. The figures in the red squares represent the player's loss in each 1000 hands. The figures in the lighter squares indicate the player's gain in each 1000 hands, should the player double down or split a pair. (Example: If the player doubles down on 8 when the dealer has a two up, he will lose **151** additional bets in each 1000 times that he does this. If a player doubles down on nine when the dealer has a two up, he will **gain 25** additional bets in each 1000 times that he plays this way. If he splits two aces when the dealer has a three, he will gain **492** additional bets in each 1000 hands. If he splits two fours when the dealer has a four, he will lose 147 additional bets in each 1000 hands.)

This chart is another way to show you exactly what happens, proving again that there is an exact way to play every hand. And again, a check with Chart A-1 will demonstrate that these figures back up the plays indicated in the Basic Strategy rules.

When playing Basic Strategy the player will split a pair **1.79** times in each 100 hands. The player will double down **9.67** times in each 100 hands. Double downs are very important: If you fail to double down when you should, you are giving money away. If you double down when you are not supposed to you are giving money away.

CHART B-12. GAIN BY DOUBLING DOWN AND SPLITTING PAIRS

	2	3	4	5	6	7	8	9	10	ACE
8	151	102	52	7	9	254	376	485	491	575
9	25	56	105	154	159	19	104	229	295	321
10	216	247	278	308	323	171	100	47	21	46
11	270	296	327	361	362	186	119	78	53	43
A2	81	42	5	53	62	264	351	359	390	525
A3	64	33	18	67	75	235	289	333	356	495
A4	58	21	23	67	80	175	278	308	326	466
A5	50	17	25	66	101	165	248	285	313	450
A6	6	37	77	140	133	45	165	210	244	327
A7	8	22	109	127	123	172	136	167	183	257
A8	164	74	42	8	0	289	418	348	289	482
A9	276	252	195	146	134	422	555	655	607	721
AA	471	492	526	550	559	382	313	292	241	255
22	23	3	30	66	66	34	78	167	175	164
33	48	14	28	70	57	42	42	102	154	136
44	226	175	147	104	138	336	273	268	312	328
66	4	36	74	121	154	9	92	178	259	243
77	77	103	141	200	237	275	6	78	105	127
88	267	283	336	370	424	570	337	85	57	125
99	17	73	104	155	114	67	123	92	135	61
XX	296	253	201	153	154	287	438	572	550	553

CHART B-13. THIS IS WHAT HAPPENS WHEN YOU DOUBLE DOWN

This chart illustrates what happens when you double down and the dealer has a three up. The left column represents the player's hand. The top column running across represents what hands you will achieve after you have doubled down. The figures in the squares indicate how many times you will receive each hand. The minus figures in the gain column show what your loss is in each 100 times you double down. (Example: If the player doubles down on A9 when the dealer has a three, it will cost him 25 additional bets in each 100 times that he plays this way. If the player doubles down on A9, he will make 17 or better 61 times in each 100 doubles. The dealer with a three up (bottom row of figures) will make 17 or better 62 times in each 100 hands.)

Also notice that the player will make very few hands when he doubles down on A2 to A5. You will only make 17 or better 37 times in each 100 times that you double.

The count column on this chart may be disregarded at this point, but when you have learned to keep track of the cards you will then sometimes double down even on A9.

The lower section of Chart B-13 illustrates what you are to expect when the dealer has a three up. One hand in four on the average, he will make 20 or more. He will only break 38 times in each 100 hands on the average.

This chart is to make you aware of the many times you will have 19 or 20, and the dealer with a three up will beat you.

CHART B-13. THIS IS WHAT HAPPENS WHEN YOU DOUBLE DOWN

	17 OR MORE	18 OR MORE	19 OR MORE	20 OR MORE	21	16 OR LESS	GAIN	COUNT
A9	61	53	45	39	6	39	-25	12
8	49	41	8			51	-10	14
A8	61	55	47	14	8	39	-7	5
A2	41	33	24	16	8	59	-4	7
A3	39	33	24	16	8	61	-3	7
A4	39	31	24	16	8	61	-2	4
A5	35	29	20	14	6	65	-2	4
A7	61	53	20	14	6	39	2	-2
A6	61	29	22	14	8	39	4	-7
9	57	49	41	8		43	6	1
10	64	57	49	41	8	36	25	-13
11	63	56	48	40	33	37	30	-17
DEALER	62	49	36	24	12	38		

WHEN DEALER HAS A THREE UP

ONE HAND IN FOUR   HE WILL MAKE 20 OR BETTER

ONE HAND IN THREE HE WILL MAKE 19 OR BETTER

HALF OF THE TIME   HE WILL MAKE 18 OR BETTER

ONE HAND IN THREE HE WILL BREAK

WHEN DEALER HAS A THREE UP, YOU CAN DOUBLE DOWN ON A6,A7,9,10,11.
IN EACH 1000 TIMES THAT YOU DOUBLE DOWN YOU WILL GAIN 134 BETS.
YOU GAIN 13 BETS IN EACH 100 DOUBLE DOWNS WHEN DEALER HAS A THREE.

CHART B-14. DEALER'S PROBABILITIES

	17 OR MORE	18 OR MORE	19 OR MORE	20 OR MORE	21	BUST
2	65	51	38	25	12	35
3	62	49	36	24	12	38
4	60	47	35	23	12	40
5	57	45	33	21	11	43
6	58	41	31	20	10	42
7	74	37	23	15	7	26
8	76	63	27	14	7	24
9	77	64	54	18	6	23
10	76	64	52	40	4	24
ACE	83	64	45	26	8	17

CHART B-14. DEALER'S PROBABILITIES

This chart illustrates the hands that the dealer will achieve on the basis of each 100 hands. The left column running up and down represents the dealer's card. The top column running across represents what the dealer will achieve as his final hand in each situation. The squares indicate how many times this will happen. (Example: If the dealer is showing a 2, he will achieve 17 or more 65 times in each 100 hands; he will make 18 or more 51 times in each 100 hands; he will make 19 or more 38 times; 20 or more 25 times; 21 12 times; and he will break 35 times.)

Or, to reduce it to its reflective terms, you can expect a dealer who has a two up to make 18 or better. When he has an ace up, you can expect him to make a hand, as he will only break 17 times in each 100 hands when he has an ace up. When he has a 7, 8, 9, or 10 up he will only break one hand in four. So, when the dealer has a large card up (7, 8, 9, X, A) you must hit until you get 17 or more, because if you stand short, you will not even win one bet in four.

CHART B-15. RULES VARIATIONS

	LAS VEGAS STRIP 1 DECK	LAS VEGAS STRIP 4 DECK	LAS VEGAS	RENO TAHOE	PANAMA	LONDON	BAHAMAS	ST. MARTIN	ARUBA CURACAO	PUERTO RICO
FOUR DECKS	-.52	-.52			-.52	-.52	-.52	-.52	-.52	-.52
TWO DECKS	-.37	*	*	*						
NO DOUBLE ON TEN	-.56									-.56
NO DOUBLE ON NINE	-.14			-.14			-.14	-.14	-.14	-.14
NO SOFT DOUBLE	-.14			-.14		-.14		-.14	-.14	-.14
HIT SOFT SEVENTEEN	-.19		-.19	-.19	-.19			-.19	-.19	
FURTHER PAIR SPLITTING	-.05							-.05	-.05	-.05
NO HOLE CARD	-.13				-.13	-.13		-.13	-.13	
DOUBLE AFTER SPLITS	+.14	*	*		+.14	+.14				+.05
DRAW TO SPLIT ACES	+.14				+.14					+.14
HOUSE ADVANTAGE	0.10	0.53	0.20	0.48	0.57	0.66	0.67	1.18	1.18	1.23

CHART B-15. RULES VARIATIONS

This chart illustrates the effect of the rules variations in different casinos. If the house rules forbid doubling down on hard ten, the player's disadvantage in being unable to do it, as the chart reveals, is -0.56%. Or if a player is able to draw to split aces, this will give him an advantage of 0.14%. Also indicated are the disadvantages when a casino employs two or four decks. This chart also demonstrates the player's advantage when he plays in different areas. In Northern Nevada (Reno-Lake Tahoe) the player can only double down on 10 and 11, and cannot double down after he has split a pair. Anywhere in Las Vegas you may double down on any two cards. The asterisk indicates that in some casinos use two decks. In Las Vegas you may double down after you split a pair, and some casinos use two decks.

CHART B-16. SOME OF THE LOSING HANDS

PLAYER WILL GET 12-13-14-15-16-17, 43.4 % OF THE TIME

THESE ARE ALL LOSING HANDS AGAINST ANY UP CARD

HAND	COMBINATIONS	LOSE	LOSS IN PERCENT
12	8446	2646	- 31.36
13	8446	2904	- 34.38
14	7240	2658	- 36.72
15	7240	2838	- 39.20
16	6033	2416	- 40.05
17	6033	1752	- 29.04
AVERAGE LOSS WHEN YOU HAVE 12 TO 17			- 35.03

CHART B-16. SOME OF THE LOSING HANDS

This chart shows you the worst hands you can get, and shows you how often you can expect to get them, and what you will lose when you do get them. This chart is provided so that you are aware of the hands that are working against you. (Example: In each 100,000 hands, the player will get twelve 8446 times, he will lose 2646 units, crediting a disadvantage of 31.36%.) In other words, this chart is to show you how many really bad hands you can anticipate getting. You should know that any time you get 12 to 17, you have a bad hand and you figure to lose. Expect it. Notice that there is very little difference in the player's loss if he has 12 or if he has 17, two bets in a hundred.

CHART B-17. SOME OF THE BAD PLAYS

PLAYERS HAND	DEALER		PLAYERS LOSS	
STAND ON 13	7	UP	17	UNITS
STAND ON 16	ACE	UP	15	UNITS
HIT 16	2	UP	17	UNITS
HIT 14	4	UP	16	UNITS
SPLIT TWO SIXES	9	UP	18	UNITS
SPLIT TWO TENS	6	UP	15	UNITS
DOUBLE ON 12	5	UP	13	UNITS
DOUBLE ON A8	2	UP	16	UNITS
HIT AA	TEN	UP	24	UNITS
HIT 88	7	UP	57	UNITS
STAND ON 88	7	UP	68	UNITS

CHART B-17. SOME OF THE BAD PLAYS

This chart illustrates some of the bad plays that you sometimes see in a casino. Doubling down on twelve when the dealer has a five is a play that only an idiot would make, but it is the best play of those plays above. This play would cost the player thirteen additional bets in each 100 times that he makes this play. To stand on sixteen when the dealer has an ace, a common practice of some players, will cost the player fifteen additional bets in each 100 times that he plays this way. Notice the enormous loss when you do not split two eights when the dealer has a seven.

CHART B-18. THE FINE POINTS OF BASIC STRATEGY

TWO UP   HIT 13 IF YOU HAVE 3 AND TEN

THREE UP   STAND ON 12 IF TWO OF YOUR CARDS ARE

                   A-3   A-6   2-6   3-6   4-8
                   A-4   2-4   3-4   4-4   5-7
                   A-5   2-5   3-5   4-5
                   (If you cannot double down)

FOUR UP   HIT 12 IF YOU HAVE 2 AND TEN

NINE UP   STAND ON 16 IF TWO OF YOUR CARDS ARE

                   A-4   3-4   4-4
                   2-5   3-5   4-5

TEN UP   STAND ON 16 IF TWO OF YOUR CARDS ARE

                   A-2   A-7   2-7   3-7   5-7
                   A-3   2-3   3-3   4-4   5-8
                   A-4   2-4   3-4   4-5   5-9
STAND ON 77   A-5   2-5   3-5   5-5   5-X

This chart completes the rules of Basic Strategy by demonstrating the fine points of play. (Example: If the dealer has a two up, the player hits 13 only if he holds a 3 and 10.) These fine points may be disregarded when first learning the basic rules. But when the basic rules have been thoroughly memorized, it will be easy to add the fine points variations to your play.

You stand on two sevens when the dealer has a ten. When the dealer has a ten up he quite likely has 20 or a bad hand. If he has 20, if you are to draw and beat him, you must draw a 7. Since you have two sevens, your chance of drawing another seven is unlikely. When you have two sevens and the dealer has a ten, you have a bad hand, but it is a small gain to stand.

CHART B-19. DIFFERENT COMBINATIONS OF 8-9-10-11

		2	3	4	5	6	7	8	9	10	ACE
8	6-2	-150	-102	-58	0	-8	-240				
	5-3	-151	-103	-45	14	26	-225				
	4-4	-172	-111	-54	8	18	-219				
9	7-2	34	64	104	137	148	-24	-100			
	6-3	20	50	104	157	148	-22	-103			
	5-4	20	54	107	169	180	-11	-108			
10	8-2	211	241	252	296	307	149	87	54	-24	-61
	7-3	212	246	285	307	318	167	110	36	-15	-47
	6-4	215	250	293	339	332	190	110	47	-23	-33
	5-5	223	255	295	347	362	188	115	54	-20	-35
11	9-2	261	269	300	340	346	166	112	71	39	19
	8-3	265	295	313	350	356	181	110	76	53	35
	7-4	269	305	343	362	366	194	118	75	61	51
	6-5	283	315	352	394	381	203	136	88	57	67

CHART B-19. DIFFERENT COMBINATIONS OF 8-9-10-11

This chart illustrates the vast difference in card combinations. When the dealer has a six: if you double down on 6-2, this would cost you 8 additional bets in each 1000 times that you played this way. If you were to double down on 5-3, you would gain 26 bets in each 1000 times that you played this way.

When the dealer has a 5, if you double down on 4-4, you will gain 8 bets in each 1000 times that you double. BUT, if you split the two fours you will lose 104 additional bets in each 1000 times that you split them (Chart B-12).

Notice the big difference when you have eleven, and the dealer has an ace up: If you play the Point Count, there are times when you would not double down with 9-2, but you would double with 6-5.

70   PLAYING BLACKJACK AS A BUSINESS

CHART B-20. YOUR WIN OR LOSS WITH EACH HAND

	A	2	3	4	5	6	7	8	9	10	WIN	%
AA	3	20	22	24	27	27	20	15	10	21	183	40.55
22	18	2	3	0	4	4	2	5	8	48	80	17.60
33	20	6	2	1	3	3	5	8	11	58	104	23.05
66	21	9	6	3	1	0	8	12	14	63	136	29.94
77	24	7	4	1	2	2	2	15	17	80	146	32.18
88	21	0	2	4	7	9	7	2	15	72	79	17.54
99	13	6	7	10	13	14	15	7	2	30	26	5.71
XX	129	454	461	467	488	505	554	567	539	1150	5313	58.71
A2	27	3	7	11	20	22	10	4	1	55	6	0.49
A3	29	2	3	11	20	21	6	3	6	68	37	3.08
A4	31	1	2	6	17	19	3	3	11	85	84	6.97
A5	34	3	0	6	11	21	2	8	16	105	130	10.80
A6	33	1	7	15	27	19	6	6	13	92	69	5.74
A7	29	13	18	30	34	37	30	12	8	74	63	5.22
A8	10	39	41	40	44	47	59	44	28	0	332	27.49
A9	10	63	62	63	66	67	75	76	55	177	714	59.20
AX	301	579	579	579	579	579	579	579	579	2039	6974	144.49
23	50	10	7	4	2	2	12	17	25	141	262	21.73
24	53	11	10	4	1	1	16	23	29	141	285	23.63
7	107	19	12	2	9	12	13	43	57	304	536	22.21
8	109	3	5	18	30	35	22	13	48	285	349	12.16
9	110	30	51	76	100	105	52	32	15	248	73	2.02
10	88	130	149	168	194	195	135	95	54	68	965	23.69
11	71	183	200	223	252	256	158	120	85	141	1547	32.05
12	379	146	145	121	90	105	148	191	237	1085	2646	31.36
13	400	196	142	123	89	102	186	226	245	1195	2904	34.38
14	359	172	142	92	76	87	199	200	233	1099	2658	36.72
15	377	167	141	110	68	89	199	229	261	1197	2838	39.20
16	318	142	121	93	70	69	172	205	220	1005	2416	40.05
17	304	74	58	33	21	5	47	182	190	837	1752	29.04
18	140	46	56	63	78	104	150	28	76	325	16	0.33
19	36	149	148	156	173	187	236	223	77	18	1330	27.55
WIN	2772	752	1028	1385	1786	1835	1104	415	332	5212	15	.0150
%	36.0	9.8	13.4	18.0	23.2	23.9	14.3	5.4	4.3	16.9	.015	.0150

THESE ARE THE HANDS THAT WIN THE MOST MONEY - IN ORDER

1	AX	9	9	17	25
2	20	10	A7	18	26
3	11	11	99	19	27
4	19	12		20	28
5	10	13		21	29
6	A9	14		22	30
7	A8	15		23	31
8	AA	16		24	32

YOU GET A BLACKJACK ONCE IN 20.7 HANDS   DEALER WILL BREAK 28.36 TIMES IN 100

CHART B-21. HOW MANY TIMES YOU WILL GET EACH HAND

	A	2	3	4	5	6	7	8	9	10
AA	18	36	36	36	36	36	36	36	36	145
22	36	18	36	36	36	36	36	36	36	145
33	36	36	18	36	36	36	36	36	36	145
66	36	36	36	36	36	18	36	36	36	145
77	36	36	36	36	36	36	18	36	36	145
88	36	36	36	36	36	36	36	18	36	145
99	36	36	36	36	36	36	36	36	18	145
XX	724	724	724	724	724	724	724	724	724	2534
A2	72	72	96	96	96	96	96	96	96	386
A3	72	96	72	96	96	96	96	96	96	386
A4	72	96	96	72	96	96	96	96	96	386
A5	72	96	96	96	72	96	96	96	96	386
A6	72	96	96	96	96	72	96	96	96	386
A7	72	96	96	96	96	96	72	96	96	386
A8	72	96	96	96	96	96	96	72	96	386
A9	72	96	96	96	96	96	96	96	72	386
AX	290	386	386	386	386	386	386	386	386	1448
23	96	72	72	96	96	96	96	96	96	386
24	96	72	96	72	96	96	96	96	96	386
7	193	170	170	170	170	193	193	193	193	772
8	224	205	205	193	205	205	229	229	229	918
9	290	265	265	265	265	265	265	290	290	1158
10	326	302	302	302	290	302	302	302	326	1303
11	386	362	362	362	362	362	362	362	362	1544
12	676	579	652	652	652	652	652	652	652	2606
13	676	676	579	652	652	652	652	652	652	2606
14	579	579	579	483	555	555	579	555	555	2220
15	579	579	579	579	483	555	555	555	555	2220
16	483	483	483	483	483	386	458	483	458	1834
17	483	483	483	483	483	483	396	458	458	1834
18	386	386	386	386	386	386	386	290	386	1448
19	386	386	386	386	386	386	386	386	290	1448

These two charts show you everything that will happen in a Black-jack game. You will be able to learn many things from these charts. In each 100,000 hands, these are the hands you will get on the average. You can see how many times you get each hand against each up card, and you will see exactly what your win or loss is. Example: You will get two aces 18 times when the dealer has an ace up, and you will lose 3 units. But overall you will get two aces 452 times and you will win 183 units. When you have two aces you will have an average advantage of 40.55%. Notice the big difference when you have X-9, or A-8, and the dealer has a ten. One hand is a winning hand and one hand is a losing hand, yet they are both 19. Notice that you will lose more money with 13 than with any other hand.

When playing on the Las Vegas Strip with typical rules, playing Basic Strategy with a single deck the house has an advantage of 0.15% This small disadvantage means: If you were to play 1000 hands, and bet one dollar each time, at the end of your playing session you would lose fifteen cents. In other words, you have an even gamble when playing Basic Strategy on the Las Vegas Strip.

This, then, is the basic framework for your approach to the game of Blackjack. With it firmly in control, you are ready to add to your playing attack the advantages of the count strategies.

But, you must continue to practice the basic strategy, because even when you are playing the count strategies, you will still play the basic strategy a majority of the time.

Most all of the people who have played for any length of time have assumed they know how to play Blackjack. But now that you have learned the material in this book, you will notice that the average Blackjack player has the wildest ideas of correct play imaginable. For example: I had a phone call from a man in Los Angeles wanting to buy one of my count strategies. I asked him if he was an experienced Blackjack player. His answer was, "I have been playing Blackjack for ten years. I know everything about the game. You hit until you get fourteen."

Another man stopped by the house. I was explaining everything to him as he wanted to become a strategy player. I told him you never take insurance unless you are counting cards. He then asked me: "If you have a Blackjack and the dealer has an ace up, would you take insurance?" When I answered, "Probably not. It would depend upon the count." He replied: "If you are that stupid, I do not even want to talk to you, that is the only sure play in Blackjack." I tried to explain to him that he would win the insurance bet less than four times in each thirteen times that he took insurance, but he would not listen. He left.

Even though this basic section in the book was written for beginners, I am certain that many players who have played for years have been able to benefit from much of the material. In this case I am gratified. The Basic Strategy is your first step to becoming a winning Blackjack player.

Chapter 6

COUNT STRATEGIES

For a long time I was convinced it was absolutely impossible for anyone to beat a Blackjack game by keeping track of cards. In the next few pages, I will show you why I changed my mind and why I turned to making my living playing Blackjack.

Since the beginning of gambling, players have tried to devise a betting strategy to overcome the house percentage. No such system has yet been invented. Keeping track of the cards is not a system. It is actually a strategy based on the mathematical theory of probabilities as certain cards are removed from the deck.

1. When large cards are removed from the deck, the house has the advantage.

2. When small cards are removed from the deck, the player has the advantage.

Probably what the average person wants is a simple system that will give him an advantage when he comes here on his vacation. To have a definite advantage, you must have a method of keeping track of the cards.

The essence of keeping track of the cards is this:

1. One-third of the time the house has an advantage that will average about 4%.

2. One-third of the time the odds are about even.

3. One-third of the time the player will have an advantage that will average about 4%.

So you need a strategy that will let you know when you have the advantage, allowing you to bet more at that time, and you need a playing strategy that will tell you how to play the hands differently at any condition of the deck. Example: if you have eleven and the dealer has a nine, and you know that in the remaining cards there is a surplus of small cards, your playing strategy would not let you double down. Or if you have twelve and the dealer has a four, and you know that in the remaining cards there is a surplus of small cards, the playing strategy would tell you to hit.

Whenever there is a surplus of small cards remaining in a deck, you bet as little as you can; the house has the advantage. The reason is simple: if the dealer has, say, a five, he figures to make a hand if the deck is full of small cards. Also, you would not double down if you figure to draw a small card, etc.

When there is a surplus of aces and tens in the remaining cards, the dealer has just as good a chance to get a good hand as the player has, BUT when the dealer gets a Blackjack he will only get paid even money. You will get paid three to two. If you each get a bad hand, you will not have to draw. The dealer must draw, and since the deck is full of large cards he will probably go busted. If the dealer gets 9-10-11 and you have a bad hand, he cannot go down for double. You can. If the dealer gets a pair and you have a bad hand, he cannot split the pair. You can. You have many advantages when the deck is rich in large cards. The dealer has only one advantage. He does get to draw last.

Not everyone can become a successful count player. My best friend has been working with me for years. He has been taught everything, and he will practice and learn the playing strategies perfectly. He cannot concentrate. He cannot keep his mind on the game. Many times, when only one hand has been dealt from the deck, he will have lost the count.

Remember by playing the Basic Strategy you have an even gamble. *Obviously then, if you keep track of the cards you have a definite advantage.* If you know that in the remaining cards there is a surplus of aces and tens, you positively have the advantage.

If you plan to make a career of playing Blackjack, and if you are to become an expert professional player, you must expect to practice for many hours. There are three important things you must do if you are to succeed.

1. You must keep track of the cards perfectly.

2. You must bet your money perfectly.

3. You must play the hands perfectly.

You do not have to have a super memory. Practice will take care of this. But you do have to be able to concentrate. You must have your mind on the game at all times.

I have discovered from teaching beginning players that they want to advance too fast. They want to learn the most difficult strategy they can find.

The Revere Plus-Minus Strategy is ideal for the beginner. The beginner must learn a simple strategy first. I suggest he learn the Basic Strategy and the Plus-Minus count. He can start to play and add the Plus-Minus playing strategy as he progresses. When he has mastered the Plus-Minus Strategy, he will win about three times in each four times that he plays.

Many system players have come to Nevada. Most of them have not been successful the first few trips. The average player comes from California, where he works or goes to school. He usually comes here on a busy weekend when the tables are full. He has been up all day and is usually tired when he starts to play. He can only be here for a short time, so he will play as many hours as he can. If he does have a bad run of luck, he will usually mismanage by betting more money than he should, and if he gets loser he will play to get even.

The average counter who comes to Nevada has practiced at home for weeks. He has never lost. When he was playing at home there were no distractions. The playing conditions were perfect. At home, if he should make a mistake, he could in fact take time and correct his mistake. But playing in the casinos is very different, there are many distractions: someone at the table is offensive; the pit boss is watching him; he does not like the dealer; he starts losing; the girl has not brought the cigarettes; the man in the last seat is a lousy player. These and many other distractions undoubtedly cause a break in concentration he did not experience at home; so when he loses his first time in actual play, his first thought is that he has been cheated.

One player from Los Angeles—his name was Bill—was a good counter. On one trip here he stayed about three weeks. He played everywhere. In that time he won $10,000. Then on the day he was planning to leave, he went to a Strip casino and he lost it all in one playing session. He came to me for advice; his first thought was that he had been cheated. I found out what really happened. He had been playing and drinking; he began losing, so he played to get even, and he drank more. No one likes to lose and no one likes to quit loser, but you must learn to do this. The systems do not always win, they just win most of the time. You must never lose more than you will win in any one playing session.

Whenever a system player loses, I believe it is because he makes mistakes; he gets loser; he gets tired; or he has learned the system perfectly, it is easy now, so he relaxes.

I have had the opportunity to watch counters from "The Eye in the Sky," the lookout overhead where a game may be watched through a one-way mirror. From that vantage point, I have seen even the best counters make unbelieveable mistakes. They made them because they allowed strain and distractions to affect their playing. This proves the necessity of always playing under the best conditions, and in a rested and prepared state of mind.

The Advanced Point Count is beautiful to play; it has so many advantages. Also, it is good for your morale to know that you are playing the most accurate strategy that has been devised. One of the most important advantages is that you will be able to play this strategy and not get barred from playing. Some (very few) pit bosses have been taught a count system (usually a simple plus-minus system). If they follow along with your play, they will see that you make plays that are different from the way they would play, so they assume that you are not a card counter.

In Las Vegas I played in one club many times. The pit boss, Joe, played the count himself, but he played a ten count system. When I played in the casino where he worked, I would play the Point Count Strategy. There is a great deal of difference between the two. The Point Count will show 50% more betting situations than the Ten Count and sometimes the Ten Count would say hit, while my strategy would say stand. Sometimes I would make a small bet and with his system he would have made a large bet. He was convinced that I played badly and that when I won it was only luck. A specific hand cinched his belief. I had a large bet up and the deck was very ten rich. I was dealt a pair of nines and the dealer had an eight showing. I knew that I should split them, but I also knew that there were no aces left in the deck and that if I stood I could not lose. The worst that could happen would be a tie, so I deliberately stood. The pit boss saw the play and walked away smiling. According to any strategy you should split two nines when the dealer has an eight even if the deck is very lean. He was happy and I was happy.

Many clubs use two or four decks. If a club is busy and I have to play with three or more players, I prefer two or four decks. I will get more hands each shuffle than from a single deck. Two or four decks are not the least bit more difficult to count than a single deck. You must watch the remaining cards so you will know exactly what the true count is. When I play with two or four decks, I prefer to play with four other players. I like to have the seat next to me vacant so that I may at times play two hands. There are advantages to play with two or four decks: the pit bosses do not watch you as closely; you can bet more freely; two and four decks will also tend to run more normal whereas a single deck will run more extreme; also, the burn or the bottom card will not be as crucial as it is with a single deck.

You must never play for more than one hour in a single club. At the end of an hour you must quit, win or lose even if the playing conditions seem to be good. If you stay longer, the bosses may see that you are counting. Always play safe. If you never lose more than thirty units in any one playing session you will never get hurt badly.

When you are playing in the casinos, many strange things will happen. Some are almost supernatural. Almost all the errors made seem to work to the advantage of the house. If a player on third base splits two tens, or hits 15 or 16 when the dealer has a small card, it always seems to help the dealer. I remember one time I was playing on a graveyard shift. It was late in the morning and the casino was deserted. There was not a person within two blocks. The deck became very good. I made two maximum bets. Just as the dealer started to deal the cards, another player put down a one dollar bet. It looked like he came out of the ceiling. Naturally, the dealer got a face card up and an ace in the hole.

I have tried to teach several women to become count players; it just doesn't seem to be their bag. They will not devote the many hours of practice required. It seems that when it comes time to practice they will always have something far more important to do. Also, they just will not believe that there is an exact way to play every hand. They want to help the system by guessing part of the time. One girl was learning the Basic Strategy. This girl was a Blackjack dealer and she had been playing for several years. The Basic Strategy tells you to split two nines when the dealer has a nine. When she saw this play on the chart she said, "I would never split two nines when the dealer has a nine." I explained to her that the Basic Strategy had been proven by electronic computer, not by one man but by many, and these men were the most brilliant mathematicians in the world. They have found that if you split two nines when the dealer has a nine, you will gain 92 additional bets in each 1000 times that you make this play. Her comment was, "I don't care, I would never split them." I do not believe the average man would think in this way.

Again, concentration is the name of the game. You must be able to visit with the pit boss, watch the entertainment, know what the player next to you has in his hand, make a date with the cocktail waitress, and still keep the count and play your hands correctly. It also requires a lot of patience to be a successful counter. You must never play unless the playing conditions are right. Many times you will have to wait for hours to find the right conditions. You must never play with a single deck when there are more than two other players. You do have an advantage, but you are better off to wait for better conditions.

After you have perfected the count and you have learned the playing strategy perfectly, then you can add refinements: learn to estimate the cards in the other player's hands when you do not see them; keep a separate count of the aces and fives. Keeping track of the aces is very important when you have a hand to double down on, and it is late in the deck. Example: You have eleven, the dealer has a ten. If the count is close you would not double down knowing that a big part of your count was made up of the aces. Or if you had ten and the dealer had a nine, even if the count told you to double, you might not double if you knew the deck was short of aces.

Chapter 7

THE REVERE FIVE COUNT STRATEGY

All gambling casinos operate with a definite advantage over the player, or they wouldn't be in business. The percentage operating in their favor, or the "edge" they have over the player, varies markedly with different games of chance. For example, the once-popular game of Faro, which has almost disappeared from the Nevada gambling scene (there is only one Faro game in Nevada), gave the player a dead even gamble as compared with Roulette, where the house has an advantage of 5 5/19 per cent.

By far, the greatest advantage the house has is at Blackjack when dealing to poor players. These players are virtually giving their money to the house. Next in line would be players with betting systems.

There have been innumerable betting systems devised by players in an attempt to overcome the casino's advantage. Perhaps the most popular, as well as the most fallacious of the systems, is the doubling up gambit known as the Small Martingale. Using this system, the player doubles his initial bet with each consecutive play until he wins, then reverts to his original bet and starts over again. Even if a player has an unlimited bankroll and his initial bet is a modest $1, and he plays in casinos where the betting limit is $500 on a single wager, you don't have to be an advanced mathematician to see that nine straight losses ($1, 2, 4, 8, 16, 32, 64, 128, 256) would by this system compel him to bet $512 on the tenth play, which the house does not allow. With each bet placed in line with this doubling-up progression, his maximum win could only be one unit, or $1 over and above his total investment in play at a given time. Other and more complicated betting systems have proven equally ineffective in challenging the casino's advantage over the player. If the house has the advantage, any betting strategy will only add to the advantage for the house.

The mathematical theory of probability has since proven that there are no betting systems or schemes for most standard gambling games which can be devised to change or alter in any way the casino's long range advantage. Craps and Roulette are games included in those which mathematicians call "Independent Trials Processes", and which are defined as games in which each play is not influenced by past outcomes or has any influence over future outcomes.

Say a deck of cards is shuffled and a single card is drawn—perhaps the Five of Diamonds—and then the card is returned to the deck which is again thoroughly shuffled. When a single card is drawn again the chance that it will be the Five of Diamonds is no greater or less than it's being any one of the other 51 cards.

It has been said that cards, like dice and the little spinning ball in Roulette, "have no memory". Blackjack, unlike other standard games falling in the category of mathematically independent trials processes, shows that cards not only have a "memory", but what happens in one round of play does influence what will happen later in the round of play and in successive rounds. Blackjack is the only casino game where winning strategies have not only been accurately devised, but put into play with a high degree of success.

In Blackjack, the composition of a deck changes during the course of play, and as it changes the advantage shifts back and forth between the player and the house. Cards which are used up on the first round of play, and are therefore missing from the deck when the second round is dealt, will shift the house advantage up or down. As each succeeding round is dealt from the depleted deck, the advantage automatically shifts back and forth between the players and the house.

With my winning strategies the player will readily know when the advantage has shifted to his favor or when the advantage has shifted to the house's favor. The player will make large bets when he has the advantage over the house, and he will make small bets when the house has the advantage.

The player will lose more of his small bets than he will win. However, since he will win the majority of his large bets, his large-bet profit will more than compensate for his small-bet loss.

A player can learn to evaluate a depleted deck of cards to determine whether or not he is confronted with a favorable or an unfavorable situation in play. For instance, should all four aces appear in the first round that is dealt, the player immediately knows that it is not possible for any ace to appear in the second round of play. He is then able to determine what is the best possible strategy to follow.

Aces play a unique part in the game of Blackjack. They are essential in forming a natural "21" and are the only cards that make "soft" hands possible (Ace 6, "soft" 17, for example). They are considered the most favorable pair for splitting which a player can be dealt. The problem of all four aces missing from the deck was solved by a high speed electronic computer. The answer was that the removal of all four aces from the deck put the Blackjack player at about a three percent disadvantage when playing Basic Strategy (2.59 to be exact). Considering how highly important aces are generally assumed to be in Blackjack, their removal from the deck did not prove to be as formidable a disadvantage to the player using Basic Strategy as might have been expected.

The computer was then required to compute the player's advantage or disadvantage when using the Basic Strategy when the deck was depleted in turn, of four twos, and then the four threes, etc. The results showed that a deck poor in nines, tens and aces lessened the player's advantage, while a deck rich in these high value cards helped him. A deck poor in lower value cards, 2 through 8, proved to be an advantage to the player, while a relative excess of them was unfavorable to him. There are a variety of winning strategies which may be based on counting one or more types of cards.

When the deck was depleted of any four cards of a kind, the greatest shift in advantage to the player over the house was caused by the removal of the four fives. Remember that when all four aces were removed from the deck, the player's disadvantage became 2.59 percent. When the deck contained no fives, the player's advantage rose to a healthy 3.04 percent. We then devised a playing strategy when we knew that all four fives were missing from the deck. With this special playing strategy we had an advantage of 3.6 percent. So you see that a winning strategy may be based on counting fives. The reason that a five has so much importance is that any time the dealer has a bad hand (12, 13, 14, 15, or 16) a five would make him a good hand. As an example, if on the first round of play all of the fives were to be dealt out, then on the next round of play the dealer has a bad hand, he cannot draw a five, he may draw another card that will bust him. Also, if you were to double down on 9, 10 or 11, if there were no fives in the deck for you to catch, you might catch a better card.

The Revere Five Count is very easy to learn. All that you keep track of is the four fives. When in the remaining cards there is a shortage of fives, the player has the advantage. Also when there is a shortage of fives you will play the hands differently.

FIVES GONE

	40-MORE	27-39	14-26	13-LESS
1	2	1	1	1
2	3	2	1	1
3	4	3	2	1
4	4	4	4	4
REMAINING CARDS	40-MORE	27-39	14-26	13-LESS

CHART C-1. BETTING STRATEGY

To play the Five Count you need to keep track of the fives, and be able to make a rough estimate of the remaining cards. You bet the amount that it says in the squares. If you are betting one or two units you play Basic Strategy. If you are betting three or four units you play the Fives Strategy. As an example: Two fives are gone, about nine cards have been dealt (43 remain). You would bet three units, and you would play your hand according to the Fives Strategy.

CHART C-2. HIT STAND

	2	3	4	5	6	7	8	9	10	ACE
12	S	S	S	S	S	H	H	H	H	H
13	S	S	S	S	S	H	H	H	H	H
14	S	S	S	S	S	H	H	H	H	H
15	S	S	S	S	S	H	H	S	S	H
16	S	S	S	S	S	H	H	S	S	H

S STAND   D DOUBLE   H HIT   P SPLIT

CHART C-3. SPLIT PAIRS

	2	3	4	5	6	7	8	9	10	ACE
AA	P	P	P	P	P	P	P	P	P	P
22	P	P	P	P	P	P	H	H	H	H
33	P	P	P	P	P	P	H	H	H	H
44	H	H	D	D	D	H	H	H	H	H
66	P	P	P	P	P	H	H	H	H	H
77	P	P	P	P	P	P	P	H	S	H
88	P	P	P	P	P	P	P	P	P	P
99	P	P	P	P	P	S	P	P	S	S
XX	S	S	S	S	P	S	S	S	S	S

CHART C-4. DOUBLE DOWN

	2	3	4	5	6	7	8	9	10	ACE
8	H	H	D	D	D	H	H	H	H	H
9	D	D	D	D	D	D	H	H	H	H
10	D	D	D	D	D	D	D	D	D	D
11	D	D	D	D	D	D	D	D	D	D
A2	H	D	D	D	D	H	H	H	H	H
A3	H	D.	D	D	D	H	H	H	H	H
A4	H	D	D	D	D	H	H	H	H	H
A5	H	H	D	D	D	H	H	H	H	H
A6	D	D	D	D	D	D	H	H	H	H
A7	D	D	D	D	D	S	S	H	H	S
A8	S	D	D	D	D	S	S	S	S	S
A9	S	S	S	S	D	S	S	S	S	S

CHART C-2, C-3, C-4.

These charts illustrate how you play the hands when you know that in the remaining cards there is a shortage of fives. The dealer's up card is represented by the top column running across. Your hand is represented by the left column running up and down. To know the situation you match your hand with the dealer's up card. The consequent square gives you the play. (Example: If you have 12 and the dealer has 6, you stand).

The betting schedule that I describe in Chart C-1 is the amount you would like to bet. Casino bosses are alert for anyone who changes the size of his bets. You never bet more than double the amount of your last bet.

1. If your last bet was one unit, your next bet, win or lose could not be more than two units.

2. If your last bet was two units, your next bet, win or lose could not be more than four units.

The Fives Count is your first step to becoming an expert strategy player. You have an advantage when you play this system, but mainly it is to teach you discipline. To be successful with this strategy, or any strategy, you must do everything perfectly. Also you must plan to practice many hours. This strategy will be a big help to you later on if you plan to play one of the more advanced strategies. Many times you will notice early in the deck there is a shortage of fives remaining. Then you may play according to this strategy instead of the strategy you are playing then.

CHART C-5. HOW TO PRACTICE

After you have learned the Basic Strategy, then learn the Fives Count Strategy. You must learn it so well that you can play each hand correctly, without hesitation. To practice use Chart B-9.

You have 12,	Dealer has 6.	You stand.
You have AA,	Dealer has 3.	You split.
You have 14,	Dealer has 3.	You stand.
You have 10,	Dealer has 9.	You double.
You have 44,	Dealer has 4.	You double
You have 13,	Dealer has 8.	You hit.
You have A8,	Dealer has 5.	You double.

It is very easy to get barred from playing Blackjack. Gambling is a serious business in Nevada. If at any time the bosses think you have an advantage over the house, they will ask you not to play any more Blackjack. If you are playing and you vary the size of your bets in any set manner where they can assume that you are keeping track of the cards, they will usually tell you in a nice way not to play, or they may ask you to leave the casino and not come in any more. This has been happening ever since there has been gambling; but years back they only barred players who were known cheaters. They can legally do this, since gambling is a privileged business in Nevada. Obviously, they will not let anyone play Blackjack if they think he has any advantage over the house. The casinos can bar you from playing or even bar you from coming into the club. This was tested in a court case at Lake Tahoe, and the court ruled in favor of the gambling industry. It does not make any difference how much money you are betting. You may be betting as little as one dollar, with a top bet of three dollars and be playing at a table where other players are betting five hundred dollars. If the bosses think you are keeping track of the cards, they will ask you not to play.

Many players were barred from playing in the past because they didn't have the accuracy that we have now. A few years ago you had to vary the size of your bets more than you do now in order to win.

To be a successful count player now you must have a very accurate system, so that you do not have to vary the size of your bets. If you will follow the playing rules that I will prescribe, it will be virtually impossible to detect you as a count player. You will appear to play like any other player at the table. You will never bet any more than double the size of your last bet.

Chapter 8

THE REVERE PLUS MINUS STRATEGY

There is more money to be made playing Blackjack than doing anything that I know. I have made as much as $50,000 in a month. I have taught several players who have made $100,000 in a year.

Blackjack is played all over the world now. If you learn to play effectively you can play in any part of the world. The rules are not as good as they are in Nevada, but you can win if you play well.

I spent most of last year in the West Indies area. I played in Antigua, in the British West Indies; Dominican Republic; St. Martin, in the Netherlands West Indies; Puerto Rico; and Nassau and Freeport in the Bahamas. My winnings averaged $1,000 an hour.

The games in other parts of the world are not always dealt as honestly as they are in Nevada. Nevada casinos have so much business that they do not have to cheat you. Any casino found cheating is immediately closed. The gambling in the West Indies is honest with the exception of Antigua. I suggest that you stay away from there.

I have had to play under some very adverse conditions here in Nevada. I recall an instance, in May 1967, when I was in Caesar's Palace. I was fooling around, playing for small stakes. The graveyard shift came to work and the pit boss recognized me. The pit boss called for the casino manager. He came in and we had a short discussion. He said that I could only play in this casino under certain conditions. The conditions were that the dealer would shuffle the deck, then burn eleven cards, and then deal only halfway through the deck before reshuffling. The casino manager stated that no one could beat the game under these conditions. I accepted the challenge. I played for seven hours and I won $18,000. I really should have won more, because at times I was playing three hands and betting as much as $500 on each hand. Evidently the casino manager learned his lesson, because after that particular play I was barred from playing in that casino under any conditions.

After you have learned the Basic Strategy, you may learn the Revere Plus Minus Strategy. Then, if you practice and keep your mind on the game, you will positively win.

In the book *Beat the Dealer* by Dr. Edward Thorp, there is a simple Plus Minus Strategy. With this system you keep a count, plus or minus, then you play the hands according to the Basic Strategy. If you bet $5 to $25 you will win $25 an hour on the average (one top bet an hour).

The Revere Plus Minus Strategy is similar to Dr. Thorp's strategy, in that small cards have a plus value as they are removed from the deck, and aces and tens are counted as minus values as they are removed from the deck. Dr. Thorp's strategy suggested you play the hands according to the Basic Strategy. The Revere Plus-Minus Strategy has a simple playing strategy that will add to your advantage.

The Revere Plus-Minus Strategy will win about the same amount as the Thorp strategy. The Revere Strategy has the advantage of a playing strategy, but I suggest you bet your money more conservatively. In each hour that is played you will wager more money with the Thorp strategy on the average, but the win rate will be almost identical.

Keeping track of the cards will be far simpler than you would ever imagine. You do not keep track of the cards as such. Each card has a value, plus, minus, or zero. With only ten minutes practice you will be able to keep track of the cards. The average person can learn the Plus-Minus Strategy in two days.

CHART D-1. THE COUNT

2-3-4-5-6   COUNT PLUS ONE AS THEY ARE REMOVED FROM THE DECK

7-8-9   COUNT ZERO

ACES-TENS   COUNT MINUS ONE AS THEY ARE REMOVED FROM THE DECK

When small cards are removed from the deck, the player has the advantage. So when you see a small card dealt from the deck, you count plus one; this is good for you. When you see an ace or a ten dealt from the deck, you count minus one because that is good for the house. At any time the count is plus, the player has the advantage. If the count is minus, the house has the advantage. We make small bets when the house has the advantage, and make larger bets when we have the advantage.

Take a deck of playing cards, turn one card over at a time, call out the value of each card. About twice through the deck and you will know the card values. Then practice by keeping a running count (adding them together). The count starts at zero, and will be zero again when all of the cards have been dealt out. Then practice by turning the cards over two at a time and counting them in pairs.

This will not be as easy as it seems. It takes a lot of concentration to keep the count, to play the hands perfectly, and to bet your money properly. You should plan to spend many hours practicing. If this were easy, everyone would be making their living playing Blackjack.

This is your first step to becoming an expert strategy player. In the Advanced Point Strategy, each card is given the exact value it has on the remaining cards as it is removed from the deck. Also, you will learn that there is an exact way to play *each* hand. You must learn this simple strategy first to get casino experience.

CHART D-2. HOW TO COUNT

DEALERS UP CARD	4	PLUS	1	
YOUR TWO CARDS	5-6	PLUS	3	
TWO HIT CARDS	3-X	PLUS	3	(YOU DOUBLE)
YOUR CARD	9	PLUS	3	
DEALERS HOLE CARD	X	PLUS	2	
DEALERS HIT CARD	X	PLUS	1	
PLAYERS OTHER CARDS	3-4	PLUS	3	

You count each card as it shows. You must get into the habit of counting the cards one way, so that you have a definite pattern.

In the above chart you are playing with the dealer and one player to your right. You start your count with the dealer's up card, then you count your two cards, the hit cards, the dealer's hole card, his hit cards, and the other player's cards as the dealer turns them over. This is called a running count. You have an up to date count at all times.

Chart D-2 represents the first hand dealt from the deck. At the end of the hand your count is plus three. The count continues to the next hand. You bet your money according to the up-to-date count.

CHART D-3. PLAYS THAT YOU WILL ALWAYS MAKE

LEARN THIS CHART FIRST. THESE ARE THE PLAYS YOU WILL ALWAYS
MAKE REGARDLESS OF THE COUNT. <u>THIS CHART IS VERY IMPORTANT</u>.

<u>WHEN YOU HAVE   12-13-14-15-16</u>

IF DEALER HAS 2-3-4-5-6 YOU ALWAYS STAND ON 15 AND 16

IF DEALER HAS 7-8-9-ACE YOU HIT UNTIL YOU GET 17

IF DEALER HAS TEN   YOU HIT UNTIL YOU GET 16

<u>WHEN YOU HAVE   9-10-11, OR A2 TO A7</u>

YOU HAVE 9   ALWAYS DOUBLE WHEN DEALER HAS 5 OR 6

YOU HAVE 10   ALWAYS DOUBLE WHEN DEALER HAS 2 THRU 7

YOU HAVE 11   ALWAYS DOUBLE WHEN DEALER HAS 2 THRU 9

YOU HAVE A3 TO A5 ALWAYS DOUBLE WHEN DEALER HAS 5 OR 6

YOU HAVE A6   ALWAYS DOUBLE WHEN DEALER HAS 3-4-5-6

YOU HAVE A7   ALWAYS DOUBLE WHEN DEALER HAS 4-5-6

<u>WHEN YOU HAVE A PAIR</u>

AA,33,77,88   YOU SPLIT THE SAME AS BASIC STRATEGY

22,66,99   BASIC UNLESS DEALER HAS 2-3-4

THIS STRATEGY IS VERY POWERFUL, BUT IT MUST
BE PLAYED CORRECTLY FOR YOU TO SUCCEED

1. YOUR COUNT MUST BE PERFECT

2. YOU MUST BET YOUR MONEY PERFECTLY

3. YOU MUST PLAY THE HANDS PERFECTLY

CHART D-4. HIT STAND

	2	3	4	5	6	7	8	9	10	ACE
12	H	S H	S H	S H	S H	H	H	H	H	H
13	S H	S H	S H	S	S	H	H	H	H	H
14	S H	S	S	S	S	H	H	H	H	H
15	S	S	S	S	S	H	H	H	H	H
16	S	S	S	S	S	H	H	H	S H	H
A7	D S	D S	D	D	D	S	S	H	H	S H

S H　STAND IF THE COUNT IS PLUS ONE OR MORE, OTHERWISE HIT.
D S　DOUBLE IF THE COUNT IS PLUS ONE OR MORE, OTHERWISE STAND.
WHEN DEALER HAS 2 THRU 6, YOU ALWAYS STAND ON 15 AND 16.

CHART D-5. SPLIT PAIRS

	2	3	4	5	6	7	8	9	10	ACE
AA	P	P	P	P	P	P	P	P	P	P
22	H	P H	P H	P	P	P	H	H	H	H
33	H	H	P	P	P	P	H	H	H	H
66	P H	P H	P H	P	P	H	H	H	H	H
77	P	P	P	P	P	P	H	H	S H	H
88	P	P	P	P	P	P	P	P	P	P
99	P S	P S	P	P	P	S	P	P	S	S

P S　SPLIT IF THE COUNT IS PLUS ONE OR MORE, OTHERWISE STAND.
P H　SPLIT IF THE COUNT IS PLUS ONE OR MORE, OTHERWISE HIT.
S H　STAND IF THE COUNT IS PLUS ONE OR MORE, OTHERWISE HIT.
AA,33,77,88 YOU SPLIT THE SAME AS BASIC STRATEGY

CHART D-6. DOUBLE DOWN

	2	3	4	5	6	7	8	9	10	ACE
62	H	H	H	H	H	H	H	H	H	H
53	H	H	H	D H	D H	H	H	H	H	H
44	H	H	H	D H	D H	H	H	H	H	H
9	D H	D H	D H	D	D	H	H	H	H	H
10	D	D	D	D	D	D	D H	D H	H	H
11	D	D	D	D	D	D	D	D	D H	D H
A2	H	H	D H	D H	D	H	H	H	H	H
A3	H	H	D H	D	D	H	H	H	H	H
A4	H	D H	D H	D	D	H	H	H	H	H
A5	H	H	D H	D	D	H	H	H	H	H
A6	D H	D	D	D	D	H	H	H	H	H
A7	D S	D S	D	D	D	S	S	H	H	S H
A8	S	S	D S	D S	D S	S	S	S	S	S

D S   DOUBLE IF THE COUNT IS PLUS ONE OR MORE, OTHERWISE STAND.
D H   DOUBLE IF THE COUNT IS PLUS ONE OR MORE, OTHERWISE HIT.
S H   STAND IF THE COUNT IS PLUS ONE OR MORE, OTHERWISE HIT.

CHART D-4, D-5, D-6. PLAYING STRATEGY

The player's hand is represented by the left column running up and down. The dealer's hand is represented by the top column running across. To know the situation, you match your hand with the dealer's up card, the consequent square gives you the play. (Example: If you have 12 and the dealer has a 2 up, you always hit.) (Example: If you have 12 and the dealer has a three up, you stand if the count is plus one or more. If the count is zero or less you hit.)

CHART D-7. PRACTICE HANDS

13 2	22 5	13 3	72 6	13 6	A2 4	66 2
44 6	A3 4	A6 3	10 9	11 9	33 3	14 2
A7 3	16 X	22 3	A8 3	A4 4	63 4	15 X
77 X	66 3	10 A	12 5	10 8	A2 5	12 6
A7 A	A8 4	A5 4	53 6	13 4	13 5	66 4
63 7	54 3	99 2	A4 3	66 4	A5 3	63 2
A8 6	14 3	12 3	99 3	A8 5	22 4	11 X
A7 2	A6 2	33 4	44 5	12 4	10 X	99 4
12 2	63 5	10 7	16 9	11 8	62 6	22 2

If you dealt hands for days some of the hands would never show up. Always use the practice charts. Use Chart D-7 to learn the problem hands. Go down the line ask yourself the questions. When you have learned this chart, practice with Chart B-9.

ANSWER THESE QUESTIONS IN THIS EXACT MANNER

13 2   You stand if the count is plus one or more.
       You hit if the count is zero or less.

44 6   You double if the count is plus one or more.
       You hit if the count is zero or less.

A7 3   You double if the count is plus one or more.
       You stand if the count is zero or less.

77 X   You stand if the count is plus one or more.
       You hit if the count is zero or less.

63 7   You always hit.

A8 6   You double if the count is plus one or more.
       You stand if the count is zero or less.

-5   -4   -3   -2   -1   0   +1   +2   +3   +4   +5

LESS   MORE

If you are to become a winning Blackjack player, you must learn slowly and surely. You must have your count perfect. You must be able to play the hands without any thought or hesitation. You can not make any mistakes and be a winner. I suggest that you learn in this manner:

1. Review the Basic Strategy. Do not attempt to learn this strategy until you have learned the Basic Strategy perfectly.

2. Practice the count until you know it perfectly and you are not bothered by any distractions.

3. Learn the Plus-Minus playing strategy. Practice with Chart B-9. Practice until you can answer the questions instantly.

4. When you think you are ready to play, play small. You can bet as little as fifty cents in some casinos. You want to play as cheaply as you can, because while you are learning you will make mistakes.

5. Bet your money in this manner:
   a. When the count is plus one or less, bet one unit.
   b. When the count is plus two or more, bet two units.
   c. If you bet two units and win, bet the four units if the count is plus two or more.
   d. Continue betting four units win or lose if the count is plus two or more.

CHART D-8. MONEY MANAGEMENT

You must bet in proportion to the money that you have. This will increase your advantage. First you determine your bankroll. For example, you start with $600. You use 25% as a playing bankroll. You now have a $150 playing bankroll. You want thirty units, so you divide by 30. You have thirty, five-dollar units. You play until you have won or lost 30 units, or until you have played for one hour, whichever comes first. If you are still fresh go to another casino and continue playing. With a $600 bankroll you will never lose more than $150 in any one playing session.

It will take you some time before you will be able to count the cards and retain the count. This is the hardest part of the system. There will be many distractions in a casino. Try not to talk. Never let your eyes leave the table. This is a discipline thing.

As I said before, you must always play within your bankroll. It is easy to see why you never play with money you cannot afford to lose. Even though you do not notice it at the time, your mind is not on the game as it should be, and your concentration is off. When you go out to play and you want to win badly, the very intensity of the desire may prevent you from doing so.

I generally play with a girl partner as I am less likely to be spotted as a counter. One girl named Hazel was something special to me. I wanted to win very badly when I played with her; but, because I tried so hard, or because of the thought of failure, I could never win in her company.

It is difficult to explain this phenomenon, but it is true. If you do not hope desperately to win but simply play as well as you are able, it seems that you always win.

You must never play unless you have perfect playing conditions.

You must never play with more than two other players.

Never play if there are any distractions.

Do not play if you do not like the dealer.

Be sure and tip the dealer.

Do not play if there are bad players at the table.

Do not play unless you can see all of the cards.

Play until you win or lose thirty units.

Never play for more than one hour in any club.

Play late at night when business is slow.

Vary your play if you notice a pit boss is watching you.

Practice the count, the playing strategy, and the betting strategy just before you start to play.

Never play with money you cannot afford to lose.

You must play in proportion to the money you have.

When you do lose, expect it. Never play to get even.

When you do lose, quit for awhile. Clear your mind up.

You must do exactly as the charts say. Never guess.

The count is the most important part. Concentrate on it.

Your mind has to be on the game at all times. This is work.

When the dealer pays you, do not touch the money until you are sure how much you are going to bet on the next hand.

Again, there are three things you must do to succeed.

1. You must keep the count perfectly.

2. You must bet your money perfectly.

3. You must play the hands perfectly.

Chapter 9

THE REVERE TEN COUNT STRATEGY

I developed my first Blackjack strategy in 1954. It was a plus minus strategy. I counted nines, tens, and aces as minus one, eights as zero, and all of the other cards plus one as they were removed from the deck. I did not know my advantage, so I only increased the size of my bets when I had a high plus count and I knew there was a surplus of aces remaining. I never doubled down unless the count was plus. I rarely hit twelve to sixteen if the dealer had a small card. If the count were just a little on the plus side I did not hit at all.

From 1955 to 1959, I spent an average of four hours a day on week days, and ten hours a day on week ends learning as much about the game as possible. Most of the time was spent dealing hands and recording the results. By 1959, I was playing a ten count strategy. This strategy was very similar to the ten count strategy that is published in this book.

I always counted forward. I never computed ratios at the table, but used codes instead. This way there was less computation during actual play. Counting forward is advantageous as there is less room for error.

I always kept a separate count of aces. As I learned more, I changed the playing strategy, but I still did not know my advantage. I would not make any large bet until the ratio was about 1.6.

In 1961, I started playing a plus minus strategy. I had a complete playing strategy for every possible situation. During the latter part of 1961, I decided that I could make more money playing Blackjack than I could working, so I quit work and devoted all of my time to making a living playing Blackjack. I usually played five days a week, about two hours a day on the average. I continued to study about thirty hours a week. I was constantly making changes in the playing strategy. Being a successful card counter then required a lot of time. I had to learn everything through trial and error.

It is hard work becoming a successful Blackjack strategy player. It will take hours of practice because you must be able to do everything automatically. If your count is not perfect, you can make a mistake playing the hands or betting your money. If you do not have the playing strategy down perfectly, you may make a mistake in betting your money, or lose the count. With the Ten Count Strategy, you should win two or three bets more than you lose in each hour that you play. If you make two mistakes an hour, you are not going to win anything.

In the past, the Ten Count Strategy was the most popular count strategy. With such a system, you kept track of the cards by counting tens (face cards and tens) and the other cards (aces through nines) separately.

A deck of cards contains fifty-two cards—16 tens and 36 non-tens. There is a ratio of $2\frac{1}{4}$ non-tens to each ten. If in the remaining cards there is a surplus of tens, the deck is "ten rich." If in the remaining cards there is a surplus of small cards, it is called a "lean deck."

The less the ratio is between tens and non-tens, the greater the advantage for the player. For example, if four small cards were removed from the deck, your count would become 32 non-tens and 16 tens or a ratio of 2.0. In other words, there are only two small cards now for each ten in the deck. When, in the remaining cards, the ratio is 2.0, the player has an advantage of 1.28 percent on the average. As the ratio of non-tens to tens decreases, the player has more of an advantage. Suppose there are 15 non-tens and 10 tens in the deck. That is a ratio of 1.5, and the player would have an advantage of 4.78 percent on the average.

Prior to the Revere Ten Count Strategy, all other ten counts that I have known instructed the player to count backwards. As an example: before any cards have been dealt, the player's count would be 36-16; then as the cards are removed from the deck, he would have to subtract. If, in the first hand dealt, there were seven non-tens and three tens used in play, the player's count would be 29-13. He then computed the ratio in order to determine how to play the hand and how much he should bet on the next hand.

The Revere Ten Count is much simpler, because you count forward instead of backward, and there are no ratios to compute. Instead of ratios, the Revere Ten Count uses codes. In the beginning, your count starts at zero. If, in the first hand dealt, there were three tens and seven non-tens, your count would be 3-7; this in turn corresponds to a code which tells you how to bet your money and how to play the hand. If you will look at Chart E-4 you will notice with a count of 3-7, you are in code five, and you bet one unit. With this easier strategy, there is less room for error on the part of the player.

CHART E-1. HIT STAND

	2	3	4	5	6	7	8	9	10	ACE
12	6	5	5	5	5	H	H	H	H	H
13	5	4	4	3	4	H	H	H	H	H
14	4	4	3	2	3	H	H	H	H	H
15	3	3	S	S	S	H	H	H	6	H
16	S	S	S	S	S	H	H	7	5	9
17	S	S	S	S	S	S	S	S	S	3
A7	*	*	D	D	D	S	S	H	H	5
77	P	P	P	P	P	P	H	H	5	H
88	P	P	P	P	P	P	P	P	8	P

STAND AT THE ABOVE CODE OR HIGHER.   * CONSULT CHART E-3.

CHART E-2. PAIRS

	2	3	4	5	6	7	8	9	10	ACE
AA	P	P	P	P	P	P	3	3	3	4
22	H	5	4	3	3	P	H	H	H	H
33	H	6	4	P	P	P	H	H	H	H
66	6	5	4	3	P	H	H	H	H	H
77	P	P	P	P	P	P	H	H	*	H
88	P	P	P	P	P	P	P	P	A 7	P
99	4	4	4	3	3	7	P	P	S	S
XX	S	S	7	6	7	S	S	S	S	S

SPLIT AT THE ABOVE CODE OR HIGHER.   * CONSULT CHART E-1.
A   READ IN REVERSE.   SPLIT AT CODE 7 OR LESS.

CHART E-3. DOUBLE DOWN

	2	3	4	5	6	7	8	9	10	ACE
8	H	H	7	6	5	H	H	H	H	H
9	5	5	4	3	3	6	H	H	H	H
10	D	D	D	D	D	2	3	4	6	7
11	D	D	D	D	D	D	3	4	4	5
A2	H	7	5	4	4	H	H	H	H	H
A3	H	6	5	4	D	H	H	H	H	H
A4	H	6	5	3	D	H	H	H	H	H
A5	H	6	4	3	D	H	H	H	H	H
A6	5	4	D	D	D	H	H	H	H	H
A7	6	5	D	D	D	S	S	H	H	*
A8	S	7	7	6	6	S	S	S	S	S
A9	S	S	8	8	8	S	S	S	S	S

DOUBLE AT THE ABOVE CODE OR HIGHER. * CONSULT CHART E-1.
NEVER SPLIT 44.   62.53,44 ARE EIGHT.

CHARTS E-1, E-2, E-3

These charts illustrate how you play the hands using the Ten Count codes. The dealer's up card is indicated by the top column running across. Your hand is represented by the left column running up and down. To know the situation, you match your hand with the dealer's up card. The consequent square gives you the play. Example: You have 12, the dealer has a 4 up. You stand if you are in code 5 or higher. You have two 8s, dealer has a 10 up. You split if you are in code 7 or less.

CHART E-4. CODE FOR THE TEN COUNT

TENS

CODE	1	2	3	4	5	6	7	8	9	X
0						4	7	10	14	17
1					3	6	9	12	15	18
2					4	8	11	14	16	19
3				1	6	10	13	15	18	20
4				4	8	12	14	17	19	22
5			0	6	11	14	17	18	21	23
6			3	9	13	16	18	20	22	24
7		0	6	12	15	18	20	22	23	25
8		4	10	14	18	20	22	23	25	26
9	1	8	13	17	20	22	23	25	26	28
10	6	12	16	20	22	24	25	26	28	29
11	11	16	20	23	25	26	27	28	29	30
12	16	20	23	25	27	28	29	30		31
13	21	24	26	28	29	30	31		32	33
14	26	28	29	31		32		33		34
15	31	32	33		34				35	
BET	1	1	1	1	1	2	3	4	5	5

OTHERS

In the Revere Ten Count you keep track of the cards by counting tens and others. The left column running up and down indicates the amount of tens that have been dealt from the deck. The numbers in the center squares indicate the number of non-tens that have been dealt from the deck. The top row of figures represents the code. The bottom row of figures running across tells you how much to bet when you are in the various codes. Example: On the first hand dealt from the deck, 5 tens and 14 non-tens were used up. Your count becomes 5-14. You then check the chart, matching the tens with the others. You look up at the top of the chart and see that you are in code 6. Now you look at the bottom of the chart and it tells you to bet two units.

CHART E-5. HOW TO PRACTICE

Use Chart B-9. Basic Strategy Chapter.

You have 12 dealer has 6. You stand if you are in code 5 or higher.
You have AA dealer has 3. You split.
You have 14 dealer has 2. You stand if you are in code 4 or higher.
You have 10 dealer has 9. You double if you are in code 4 or higher.
You have 44 dealer has 6. You double if you are in code 5 or higher.
You have 22 dealer has 3. You split if you are in code 5 or higher.

CHART E-6. THE PLAYER'S ADVANTAGE

CODES	AVERAGE RATIO TENS-OTHERS	PLAYERS ADVANTAGE IN PERCENT
1-4	2.35 UP	- 3.04
5	2.28	0.25
6	1.90	1.91
7	1.70	3.25
8	1.50	4.78
9	1.30	6.33
X	1.10	8.37

Chart E-6 illustrates the player's advantage or disadvantage in the various codes. The chart also shows you what the average ratio is for each code. Example: On the first hand dealt from the deck, 3 tens and 10 non-tens were dealt from the deck. You check with Chart E-4 and find you are in code 6. The above chart tells you that in code 6, your average ratio is 1.90, and that you have an average advantage of 1.91 percent.

CHART E-7. DIFFERENT BETTING STRATEGIES

	1-4	5	6	7	8	9	X	EACH 100 HANDS	%
PERCENT	-3.04	0.25	1.91	3.25	4.78	6.33	8.37		
1-2	$5	$5	$10	$10	$10	$10	$10	$16.79	2.61
1-3	5	5	10	15	15	15	15	23.89	3.18
1-4	5	5	10	15	20	20	20	29.37	3.58
1-5	5	5	10	15	20	25	25	33.14	3.84
1-6	5	5	10	15	20	25	30	35.13	3.98

CHART E-7. DIFFERENT BETTING STRATEGIES

This chart illustrates what you win when you bet your money in various ways. The top column running across indicates the code. Each of the codes represents an average ratio (code 6 the average ratio is 1.90). The second column running across indicates your advantage when you are in the various codes (code 7 your average advantage is 3.25%). The left column running up and down indicates how you vary your bets. (1-2 indicates that you spread your bets from one to two). When you vary your bets from one to two, you bet $5 if the house has the advantage, and you bet $10 when the player has the advantage. If you play in this manner you will win $16.79 an hour on the average. You will have an average advantage of 2.61 percent over the house. If you can spread your bets from one to six, you will win $35.13 an hour on the average, and you will have an average advantage of 3.98 percent. This is the way that you would like to bet your money, but you cannot bet in this manner. If your last bet was two units, your next bet could not be more than four units, win or lose.

Whenever the dealer has an ace as his up card the player may take insurance. Insurance is a side bet. When the player takes insurance, he is betting that the dealer will have a ten or a face card in the hole, thereby giving the dealer a Blackjack.

You may take insurance in any Las Vegas casino, in about half of the casinos in Reno and Lake Tahoe, and in most of the other casinos throughout the world. Insurance is usually a very bad bet.

As an example: You are playing at a table with only you and the dealer. On the first hand dealt, the dealer has an ace as his up card. If you do not look at your hand there are fifty-one unseen cards. Sixteen are ten value cards and thirty-five are non-tens. The odds are 35-16 that the dealer does not have a Blackjack. If you take insurance the house will pay you at odds of only two to one. This would give the house an advantage of about 6%. It is even a worse bet to take insurance if you hold a Blackjack yourself, then there would be forty-nine unseen cards. Fifteen tens and thirty-four non-tens. Then the odds would be 34-15, and this would give the house an advantage of about 8%. If you hold two tens and take insurance the odds are 35-14, giving the house an advantage of about 14%.

The insurance bet is bad for ordinary players, but if you are playing any of the count strategies, insurance is very important. The count player will take insurance when he knows that in the remaining cards there is a surplus of tens, when the dealer is more likely to have a Blackjack.

When you are playing the Ten Count Strategy you will take insurance only when the ratio of non-tens to tens is 2.0 or less.

When you are playing the Point Count Strategy you will take insurance if the true count is plus two or more. When the true count is plus two or more, your average ratio is 2.0 or less.

CHART E-8. SHORT CODE FOR THE TEN COUNT

CODE	2	4	6	8	X
2			8	14	19
3		1	10	15	20
4		4	12	17	22
5		6	14	18	23
6		9	16	20	24
7	0	12	18	22	25
8	4	14	20	23	26
9	8	17	22	25	28
10	12	20	24	26	29
11	16	23	26	28	30
12	20	25	28	30	31
13	24	28	30	31	33
14	28	31	32	33	34

CHART E-8. SHORT CODE FOR THE TEN COUNT

After you have generally learned Chart E-4, then you can learn this chart for actual play. I have left out half of the codes to make it easier to learn. If the count is 6-18, you would be in between code six, and code eight. You would be in code seven. When I played the Ten Count I wrote this code inside the top of a cigarette package. Later I had it engraved on a cigarette lighter. The lighter would be in front of me at all times when I played. I could look at it anytime and see what the code was. I had absolute accuracy. The engraving was small. No one else was aware that the system was on the cigarette lighter.

Many mechanical gadgets were devised by other players to keep the count and figure ratios for the ten count strategies. Dr. Thorp sold one, he called it "The Beat the Dealer Computer." It worked well, and it was useful to practice with, but it was too bulky to use at the Blackjack tables in the casinos.

CHART E-9. THE BURN CARD

	3.75	3.22	2.80	2.45	2.17	1.92	1.71	1.53	1.37
39	3.88	3.33	2.90	2.55	2.25	2.00	1.78	1.60	1.44
	4.44	3.78	3.22	2.80	2.45	2.17	1.92	1.78	1.60
	3.17	2.70	2.55	2.33	2.12	1.94	1.78	1.63	1.50
26	3.33	3.00	2.71	2.49	2.25	2.06	1.90	1.74	1.60
	4.00	3.55	3.17	2.85	2.57	2.33	2.12	1.95	1.78
	3.00	2.63	2.43	2.20	2.00	1.82	1.67	1.53	1.40
13	3.33	3.00	2.71	2.47	2.25	2.06	1.89	1.74	1.60
	5.00	4.33	3.80	3.33	3.00	2.69	2.43	2.20	2.00

CHART E-9. THE BURN CARD

The center line is the ratio that your count tells you have. But, your true ratio is either the top or the bottom line. If you do not see the burn or the bottom card you need a ratio of 1.6 to have a sure advantage when 13 cards remain. Example: You have a ratio of 2.06 and 13 cards remain. If you do not know what the burn or the bottom card is, your true ratio is 1.82 or 2.69.

This is the same with the Plus Minus Strategy. Your count may show that you have a 3% advantage. But, if you have not seen the burn or the bottom card, you may not have an advantage.

Any time you have not seen the burn or the bottom card, and it is late in the deck, if you have a close decision: think, reason, be conservative.

The Revere Ten Count Strategy was included in the book merely to show you what the Ten Count Strategy was, and how we originally had to play. I do not recommend that anyone learn the Ten Count. The Plus-Minus Strategies are easier to learn and are far more powerful.

Chapter 10

THE REVERE
POINT COUNT STRATEGY

The game of Blackjack can be mastered only by going through a step by step process of learning. My intention is to guide either the novice or the seasoned player through this process as simply and effectively as possible. The final stage of this process is the Revere Point Count Strategy.

In my strategies I have left out some of the extreme situations. I never would double down on six or seven. This play looks too bad. A bad player may hit sixteen when the dealer has a five but he would never double down on six or seven. I also play very carefully when the dealer has a two. When you are counting cards, eights and nines have very little value. The deck may have a surplus of eights and nines at any time and you would not be aware of it. I always assume that the deck has a surplus of eights and nines when they can harm me. I never double down with eight when the dealer has a two, and I rarely soft double down when the dealer has a two.

Overall you are better off to play one hand. This looks more natural. However, if I have bet three or more units and I have won, and if it is still early in the deck, then I will divide the money and play two hands if the count is right. You have to be careful not to do anything that the ordinary player would not do. There are only a few pit bosses who know anything about the count, but they will notice if you do anything that is unusual, such as changing the size of your bets. You may parlay your money, this looks natural, but do not make a large bet from the money in front of you. Play safe at all times. If you get barred from playing you are out of business. Never over bet. Your disadvantage may be more than your advantage.

There has never been a blackjack strategy available that is as accurate and as powerful as the Revere Point Count. This strategy was devised from computer runs by Julian Braun. It required more than 192,000,000 computer dealt hands to perfect this strategy.

However, if you were to pay $10,000 for a Blackjack system it would not benefit you in any way unless you were willing to study and practice for the time necessary to master it. Furthermore, the most important thing is that you practice properly.

Remember, if you play Basic Strategy you have an even gamble. So, obviously, if you keep track of cards and make no mistakes you will positively win. But, you are better off to play Basic Strategy and make no mistakes than to play a count strategy and make mistakes.

If you are to become a winning blackjack player you must learn slowly and surely. There is no easy way. If you will follow the rules I suggest, and follow them religiously, you can be successful.

You MUST learn the Basic Strategy first. I have pointed this out many times in the book but this point does not seem to get across to the reader. I have never had anyone come to me for consultation who knew the Basic Strategy perfectly.

Basic Strategy is so very important for this reason: as soon as you are dealt each hand you will immediately be able to anticipate what you will probably do. You will not make any dumb plays, and your mind will be free to keep the count and observe other things. You will play Basic Strategy eighty percent of the time.

I strongly advise against learning the Point Count strategy first. Believe me! You must learn in steps! You are not going to succeed unless you do.

Learning how to play blackjack is like starting to school. You do not start the first grade by learning algebra before you have learned simple arithmetic.

As I mentioned before: The beginner is always in a hurry, he wants to get to the most complicated strategy as fast as possible.

If you are to be successful you must learn the simple Plus-Minus strategy first. This has an easy count. You will learn to keep the count, you will learn not to be distracted by the various things that happen in the casinos, and you will be able to master this simple playing strategy. Most important, you will be able to play this easy strategy and win. If you start with a more complicated strategy you may never be able to play it well enough to win.

After you have learned your strategy and you are playing in the casinos you must continue to practice. You do not get the proper practice when you are playing in the casinos.

I know of many players who have failed merely because they quit practicing their playing strategies. When playing in the casinos some of the hands will come up so infrequently that you will forget how to play these unusual hands.

You do get practice with the count when you are playing in the casinos, but, you may be making mistakes and not be aware of it.

Every day you must practice:

1. Review the Basic Strategy. Use Chart B-9.

2. Practice the count. Use Chart F-3.

3. Practice the playing strategy. Use Chart B-9.

TO MASTER THE POINT COUNT
YOU MUST LEARN IN THIS EXACT MANNER:

1. Practice the Basic Strategy with Chart B-6. Go over and over the questions until the answers become automatic.
   Do nothing until these questions require no more thought than walking across the room. It has to be this way.

2. Read the book several times! You will have missed many important points. Study the charts in the Basic Strategy Chapter. Every chart is there for a reason. Learn why you make every play. Understand everything about the game.

3. Practice the Basic Strategy with Chart B-8 and B-9. Practice until you can go down the line and answer the questions without even a slowdown. Knowing the answers is not enough. You must be able to answer the questions automatically. After you have learned the Basic Strategy the rest is simple.

4. Learn the Revere Plus-Minus Strategy. After learning the Basic Strategy this will be easy. Play this strategy for several weeks until you can keep the count and you are not bothered by the distractions in the casinos. Learning this simple strategy will teach you the close decisions which are the most important plays. When this strategy becomes easy for you to play learn the true count in the Point Count Chapter. Then bet your money according to the true count.

5. You are now ready to learn the Point Count. The most important part to concentrate on is the two card combinations. When playing any of the count strategies, the count is most important. When your count is inaccurate you have nothing.

CHART F-1. THE COUNT

2-7   COUNT PLUS ONE AS THEY ARE REMOVED FROM THE DECK

3-4-5-6   COUNT PLUS TWO AS THEY ARE REMOVED FROM THE DECK

8-9   COUNT ZERO

ACES-TENS   COUNT MINUS TWO AS THEY ARE REMOVED FROM THE DECK

CHART F-2. HOW TO COUNT

DEALERS UP CARD	4	PLUS 2	
YOUR TWO CARDS	5-6	PLUS 6	
TWO HIT CARDS	3-X	PLUS 6	(YOU DOUBLE)
YOUR CARD	9	PLUS 6	
DEALERS HOLE CARD	X	PLUS 4	
DEALERS HIT CARD	X	PLUS 2	
PLAYERS OTHER CARDS	3-4	PLUS 6	

You count each card as it shows. You must get into the habit of counting the cards in this way, so that you have a definite pattern.

In the above chart, you are playing with the dealer and one player to your right. You start your count with the dealer's up card, then you count your two cards, the hit cards, the dealer's hole card, his hit cards, and the other player's cards as the dealer turns them over. This is called a running count. It gives you an up to date count at all times.

Chart F-2 represents the first hand dealt from the deck. At the end of the hand your count is plus six. The count continues to the next hand. You bet your money according to the up to date count.

KEEP A SEPARATE COUNT OF ACES

Later, after you have played for some time you will keep a separate count of the aces. You will do this for these reasons.

1. If there is a shortage of aces in the remaining cards you would hit less than your true count told you to hit. Your true count would be misleading, as there would be a surplus of tens in the remaining cards.

2. If there is a surplus of aces in the remaining cards you would hit more than your count told you to hit.

3. On a close decision you would not double down on eleven if you knew there was a surplus of aces.

4. On a close decision you would not double down on ten if you knew there was a shortage of aces in the remaining cards.

5. On a close decision you would not take insurance if there was a surplus of aces.

WHEN TO TAKE INSURANCE

Insurance pays two to one. When the dealer has an ace showing and you know that in the remaining cards one third or more are tens, you take insurance. You take insurance when the true count is plus 2 or more, IF THERE IS AN EQUAL DISTRIBUTION OF ACES. An unequal distribution of aces will cause drastic changes.

As an example: Dealer has ace, 13 cards remain.
    Take insurance at minus 4 if 0 aces remain.
    Take insurance at plus 2 if 1 ace remains.
    Take insurance at plus 9 if 2 aces remain.

CHART F-3. PRACTICE THE TWO CARD COMBINATIONS

A-2	8-X	3-5	X-X	5-9	4-X	A-5
8-X	5-7	A-6	8-9	2-3	3-X	4-X
3-9	X-X	4-9	7-X	7-X	6-9	A-X
4-6	X-X	2-9	X-X	3-6	A-9	3-X
A-9	6-X	A-9	A-4	X-X	2-7	A-3
2-8	X-X	5-6	6-X	5-6	A-6	2-6
4-5	8-X	2-X	7-X	7-9	5-X	5-X
A-4	6-7	3-7	8-X	3-7	X-X	4-8
8-X	8-X	4-9	X-X	7-7	2-2	6-9
4-7	4-X	A-8	5-8	6-X	X-X	2-7
6-9	3-5	5-7	X-X	2-5	X-X	X-X
3-6	X-X	3-X	8-X	9-X	3-5	9-X
2-X	X-X	3-4	A-6	3-5	3-X	6-8
X-X	2-7	2-6	4-X	6-8	X-X	8-9
3-X	8-X	A-5	A-X	A-7	4-X	3-8
5-X	3-4	2-3	X-X	2-4	X-X	7-X
X-X	8-9	4-6	3-X	4-X	2-7	2-7
X-X	A-5	2-5	2-8	X-X	4-5	A-2
3-X	4-7	8-X	9-X	7-8	5-X	5-X
5-X	6-X	9-X	4-9	6-7	3-X	A-6
6-X	2-5	X-X	4-X	5-9	A-X	7-X
A-X	3-7	X-X	7-8	4-8	6-X	2-3
2-9	A-2	A-9	A-4	A-8	9-X	X-9

CHART F-3. PRACTICE THE TWO CARD COMBINATIONS

As the dealer turns the hands over he will turn the cards over two at a time. You must learn to count them at a glance. Do not think of A-2 as minus 2 and plus 1, but as minus 1. Do not think of 8-X as zero and minus 2, but as minus 2. Practice by going over and over this chart until you look at any two cards and get the total automatically. Start at the top left corner. Go down the lines. Continue the count from one line to another. This will take you from plus into minus, etc. When you have counted the entire chart your count will be zero.

CHART F-4. HIT STAND

	2	3	4	5	6	7	8	9	10	ACE
12	+3	+2	0	-2	-1	H	H	H	H	H
13	0	-1	-3	-5	-4	H	H	H	H	H
14	-3	-4	-5	S	S	H	H	H	H	H
15	-6	S	S	S	S	H	H	H	+5	H
16	S	S	S	S	S	H	H	+7	0	H
A7	*	*	D	D	D	S	S	H	H	-2
77	P	P	P	P	P	P	H	H	0	H
88	P	P	P	P	P	P	P	P	+5	P

IF THE TRUE COUNT EQUALS OR EXCEEDS THE ABOVE NUMBER, STAND.
* CONSULT CHART F-6

CHART F-5. SPLIT PAIRS

	2	3	4	5	6	7	8	9	10	ACE
AA	P	P	P	P	P	P	P	P	P	P
22	H	+2	-2	P	P	P	H	H	H	H
33	H	+5	-5	P	P	P	H	H	H	H
66	+2	+1	-1	-4	-6	H	H	H	H	H
77	P	P	P	P	P	P	H	H	*	H
88	P	P	P	P	P	P	P	P	(5)	P
99	0	-3	-4	-6	-5	+6	P	P	S	+4
XX	S	S	+5	+4	+4	S	S	S	S	S

IF THE TRUE COUNT EQUALS OR EXCEEDS THE ABOVE NUMBER, SPLIT.
* CONSULT CHART F-4.   NEVER SPLIT 44.   62,53,44 ARE EIGHT.
88 vs 10, SPLIT IF THE COUNT IS LESS THAN +5.

CHART F-6. DOUBLE DOWN

	2	3	4	5	6	7	8	9	10	ACE
8	H	H	+6	+3	+3	H	H	H	H	H
9	+1	0	-2	-4	-5	+3	H	H	H	H
10	D	D	D	D	D	-6	-3	-1	+4	+3
11	D	D	D	D	D	D	-6	-4	-3	-1
A2	H	+5	+1	-3	-4	H	H	H	H	H
A3	H	+5	-1	-5	D	H	H	H	H	H
A4	H	+3	-2	D	D	H	H	H	H	H
A5	H	+3	-2	D	D	H	H	H	H	H
A6	0	-3	D	D	D	H	H	H	H	H
A7	+1	-1	D	D	D	S	S	H	H	*
A8	S	+4	+2	+1	0	S	S	S	S	S
A9	S	S	+7	+5	+5	S	S	S	S	S

IF THE TRUE COUNT EQUALS OR EXCEEDS THE ABOVE NUMBER, DOUBLE.
* CONSULT CHART F-4.

CHART F-4, F-5, F-6.   PLAYING STRATEGY

The player's hand is represented by the left column running up and down. The dealer's hand is represented by the top column running across. To know the situation, you match your hand with the dealer's up card, the consequent square gives you the play. (Example: If you have a 12 and the dealer has a 7 up, you always hit.) (Example: If you have 12 and the dealer has a three up, you stand if the true count is plus two or more. If the true count is plus one or less, hit.)

CHART F-7.   PRACTICE HANDS

44 6	22 5	13 3	72 6	13 6	A2 4	77 X
A7 A	A3 4	A6 3	10 9	11 9	33 3	14 2
66 2	16 X	22 3	A8 3	A4 4	63 4	15 X
A7 3	66 3	10 A	12 5	10 8	A2 5	12 6
16 9	A8 4	A5 4	63 7	13 4	13 5	66 4
88 X	54 3	99 2	A4 3	66 4	A5 3	63 2
A8 6	14 3	12 3	99 3	A8 5	22 4	11 X
A7 2	A6 2	33 4	44 5	12 4	10 X	99 4
12 2	63 5	10 7	53 6	11 8	62 6	22 2

If you dealt hands for days some of the hands would never show up. Always use the practice charts. Use Chart F-7 to learn the problem hands. Go down the line ask yourself the questions. When you have learned this chart, practice with Chart B-9.

ANSWER THESE QUESTIONS IN THIS EXACT MANNER

44 6   You double if the count is plus 3 or more.
       You hit if the count is plus 2 or less.

A7 A   You stand if the count is minus 2 or more.
       You hit if the count is minus 3 or less.

66 2   You split if the count is plus 2 or more.
       You hit if the count is plus 1 or less.

A7 3   You double if the count is minus 1 or more.
       You stand if the count is minus 2 or less.

16 9   You stand if the count is plus 7 or more.
       You hit if the count is plus 6 or less.

88 X   You split if the count is less than plus 5.
       You stand if the count is plus 5 or more.

EVERYTHING IS THE TRUE COUNT

-5   -4   -3   -2   -1   0   +1   +2   +3   +4   +5

LESS   MORE   →

CHART F-8. THE TRUE COUNT

COUNT				
1	½		1	2
2	1	1½	2	4
3	1½	2	3	6
4	2	3	4	8
5	2½	3½	5	10
6	3	4	6	12
7	3½	5	7	14
8	4	5	8	16
REMAINING CARDS	52	39	26	13

When you have a running count of plus or minus four, it does not necessarily mean that the correct count is plus or minus four. It depends upon the remaining cards. We base our count on half a deck, where you play a majority of the hands. This is the true count. If four small cards are removed from a complete deck, it does not affect the remaining cards as much as the removal of four small cards from half a deck. In Chart F-8, if you have a count of plus four, your true count would be plus two at the start of the deck. If a quarter of the deck is gone, your true count would be plus three. If three quarters of the deck is gone, the true count would be plus eight.

You must know the true count at all times. This will be easy, as you will only need to estimate the remaining cards within a quarter of a deck. You will bet your money and play the hands according to the true count.

CHART F-9. YOU BET YOUR MONEY IN PROPORTION TO THE ADVANTAGE YOU HAVE

COUNT	LAS VEGAS STRIP ONE DECK		LAS VEGAS STRIP FOUR DECKS		LAS VEGAS CITY		RENO-TAHOE		PANAMA		BAHAMAS		PUERTO RICO	
	ADV.	BET	ADV.	BET	ADV.	BET	ADV.	BET	ADV.	BET	ADV.	BET	ADV.	BET
ZERO	-0.01	1	-0.53	1	-0.20	1	-0.48	1	-0.57	1	-0.67	1	-1.23	1
PLUS 1	0.51	3	0.04	2	0.32	2	0.04	2	0.00	2	-0.14	1	-0.66	1
PLUS 2	1.05	4	0.61	3	0.86	3	0.58	3	0.57	3	0.47	2	-0.09	1
PLUS 3	1.59	5	1.17	4	1.40	4	1.12	4	1.13	4	1.03	3	0.47	3
PLUS 4	2.15	3-3	1.74	5	1.96	5	1.68	5	1.70	5	1.60	4	1.04	4
PLUS 5	2.71	4-4	2.31	3-3	2.52	4-4	2.23	3-3	2.27	3-3	2.17	5	1.61	5
PLUS 6	3.28	5-5	2.88	4-4	3.09	5-5	2.81	4-4	2.84	4-4	2.74	4-4	2.18	3-3
PLUS 7	3.87	6-6	3.44	5-5	3.68	6-6	3.41	5-5	3.40	5-5	3.30	5-5	2.74	4-4
PLUS 8	4.48	6-6	4.01	6-6	4.29	6-6	4.01	6-6	3.97	6-6	3.87	6-6	3.31	5-5
PLUS 9	5.11	6-6	4.58	6-6	4.92	6-6	4.64	6-6	4.54	6-6	4.34	6-6	3.88	6-6

THE ONLY WAY YOU CAN INCREASE THE SIZE OF YOUR BETS IS WHEN YOU PARLAY YOUR MONEY. NEVADA CASINOS ARE ALERT FOR PLAYERS WHO CHANGE THE SIZE OF THEIR BETS, BUT A PARLAY LOOKS NATURAL. (3-3 PLAY TWO HANDS.)

YOU BET ONE UNIT WHEN THE HOUSE HAS THE ADVANTAGE. YOU BET TWO OR MORE UNITS WHEN YOU HAVE THE ADVANTAGE.

IF YOU BET 2 UNITS AND WIN YOUR NEXT BET WILL BE 4 UNITS OR LESS. YOU BET IN PROPORTION TO YOUR ADVANTAGE.
IF YOU BET 3 UNITS AND WIN YOUR NEXT BET WILL BE 3-3 UNITS OR LESS. YOU BET IN PROPORTION TO YOUR ADVANTAGE.
IF YOU BET 4 UNITS AND WIN YOUR NEXT BET WILL BE 4-4 UNITS OR LESS. YOU BET IN PROPORTION TO YOUR ADVANTAGE.
IF YOU BET 6 UNITS AND WIN YOUR NEXT BET WILL BE 6-6 UNITS OR LESS. 6-6 IS THE MOST YOU WILL EVER BET.
IF YOU BET 2 UNITS OR MORE AND LOSE, YOUR NEXT BET WILL BE THE SAME AMOUNT OR LESS. WHATEVER THE ADVANTAGE.

WHEN YOU BET YOUR MONEY IN PROPORTION TO THE ADVANTAGE YOU HAVE IT WILL INCREASE YOUR OVERALL ADVANTAGE.

CONSULT THIS CHART BEFORE YOU PLAY IN ANY AREA. KNOW IN ADVANCE HOW YOU ARE GOING TO BET YOUR MONEY.

CHART F-10. DIFFERENT WAYS OF BETTING

SPREAD	ZERO OR LESS	PLUS 2	PLUS 4	PLUS 6	PLUS 8	PLUS X	WIN EACH HOUR
1--2	$ 5	$10	$10	$10	$10	$10	$20.60
1--3	5	10	15	15	15	15	32.61
1--4	5	10	15	20	20	20	40.59
1--5	5	10	15	20	25	25	46.98
1--6	5	10	15	20	25	30	50.98

This chart shows you exactly what happens when you bet your money in different ways. (This is with the true count) I do not suggest that you make your bets in this manner. This chart is only to make you aware of what would happen if you could bet this way. You win more money when you spread your bets from one to six, but don't forget you are also betting more money. Your gain is only 1% more than a spread of one to three. When you bet in the manner that I suggest, that is, you parlay your money, sometimes you will bet 6-6. This is a spread of one to twelve, yet it is not noticeable.

THE FINE POINTS OF PLAY

Learn the Fine Points of Basic Strategy, page 68. You will always play this way on the first hand dealt from a single deck when you see no other cards. Many of these plays will be contrary to the count.

When the rules allow the dealer to hit soft seventeen, stand on A7 vs ace at plus one or higher.

CHART F-11. THE TIMES THE DEALER WILL BREAK

	-15	-10	- 5	ZERO	+ 5	+10	+15
2	28	30	33	35	38	41	44
3	28	31	34	38	42	46	51
4	29	32	36	40	45	50	56
5	31	35	39	43	48	53	58
6	33	36	39	42	45	49	52
7	25	26	26	26	26	25	24
8	24	25	25	24	23	21	19
9	24	25	24	23	22	20	18
10	22	22	22	21	20	19	17
ACE	8	10	11	12	12	13	13

CHART F-11. THE TIMES THE DEALER WILL BREAK

This chart will show you the amount of times the dealer will break at each count, in each 100 hands. The left column running up and down represents the dealers up card. The top row running across indicates the count. Notice that the count has very little effect upon the times the dealer will break when he has a seven. When dealer has a ten, he will break most when the count is minus twelve. When the dealer has an ace, he will break most when the count is plus thirteen.

CHART F-12. GAIN BY DRAWING — TRUE COUNT PLUS TEN

	2	3	4	5	6	7	8	9	TEN	ACE
12	-10	-15	-20	-22	-16	18	19	15	14	16
13	-21	-28	-33	-36	-30	7	8	9	4	6
14	-30	-37	-43	-47	-39	0	6	2	- 2	0
15	-35	-43	-50	-53	-45	1	3	0	- 4	- 2
16	-40	-48	-55	-59	-47	0	1	- 2	- 6	- 5
17	-56	-64	-72	-72	-70	-47	-13	-15	-18	-23

CHART F-12. GAIN BY DRAWING — TRUE COUNT PLUS TEN

This chart illustrates the player's gain by drawing as opposed to standing with hard totals, when the true count is plus ten.

The left column running up and down represents the player's hand. The top column running across represents the dealer's up card. The squares indicate the result of drawing, instead of standing. The plus figures indicate the number of bets a player will gain in each 100 draws. The minus figures indicate the number of bets a player will lose in each 100 draws. (Example: If the player's hand is 13 and he draws to it when the dealer shows a 3, he will lose 28 bets in each 100 draws.)

Compare this chart with Chart B-10. In Chart B-10 the count is zero.

CHART F-13. THE PLAYER'S ADVANTAGE

	-15	-10	-.5	ZERO	+5	+10	+15
2	- 3.39	- 1.69	2.85	9.77	18.25	26.96	37.92
3	- 4.37	- 1.95	4.09	13.36	24.44	37.84	53.28
4	- 4.10	- 0.64	6.87	18.00	30.77	47.04	64.87
5	- 2.45	- 2.66	11.45	23.22	36.49	52.88	70.59
6	- 0.05	5.17	13.53	23.86	35.17	49.24	64.60
7	4.35	6.48	9.97	14.35	19.74	26.46	36.99
8	- 1.38	- 0.23	1.86	5.39	9.77	15.56	22.95
9	- 6.04	- 6.40	- 6.06	- 4.32	- 1.62	2.19	7.42
10	-11.63	-14.08	-16.01	-16.94	-16.81	-15.72	-14.22
ACE	-28.91	-32.37	-34.83	-36.04	-36.44	-35.88	-34.68
ADV.	- 5.08	- 4.54	- 2.70	-.0150	2.71	5.77	8.65

CHART F-13. THE PLAYER'S ADVANTAGE

This chart shows you the player's advantage or disadvantage with various counts. The dealer's up card is indicated by the left column running up and down. The count is indicated by the top column running across. Notice that if the deck is very negative, the best card the dealer can have for the player is a seven. When the deck is very rich, the player has the advantage unless dealer has a ten or ace. The bottom row shows your overall advantage with each count.

CHART F-14. GAIN BY DOUBLING DOWN AND SPLITTING PAIRS

This chart shows you the player's gain or loss when he doubles down or splits a pair when the true count is plus ten. This chart is similar to Chart B-12. In Chart B-12 the count is zero.

CHART F-14. GAIN BY DOUBLING DOWN AND SPLITTING PAIRS WHEN THE TRUE COUNT IS PLUS TEN

	2	3	4	5	6	7	8	9	10	ACE
8	16	92	184	246	220	17	272	498	527	400
9	154	245	326	379	360	212	84	156	307	141
10	342	423	481	522	511	389	309	202	59	170
11	400	463	514	546	523	348	268	207	163	262
A2	18	72	151	208	168	258	394	417	438	398
A3	34	58	153	199	176	354	360	427	437	390
A4	34	71	157	201	156	206	360	410	462	379
A5	20	76	159	204	184	194	335	405	433	376
A6	49	139	220	279	236	0	228	315	356	271
A7	181	272	342	360	236	62	116	224	272	180
A8	33	163	213	248	224	65	239	262	250	253
A9	22	86	163	306	183	111	272	419	417	360
AA	699	735	763	784	791	716	650	608	534	648
22	49	143	178	253	211	84	53	251	162	101
33	14	106	179	218	156	56	130	192	268	209
44	191	74	16	12	128	691	550	468	495	752
66	47	126	196	247	242	91	230	349	404	324
77	140	217	289	352	385	433	22	116	225	100
88	352	422	502	547	629	865	484	50	83	204
99	209	315	366	415	343	70	302	228	83	36
XX	8	96	172	215	176	72	231	412	411	363

CHART F-15. THE PLAYER'S ADVANTAGE WITH EACH
COUNT—FOUR DECKS

PLUS	1	+ 0.04 %		MINUS	1	- 1.08 %
PLUS	2	+ 0.61 %		MINUS	2	- 1.62 %
PLUS	3	+ 1.17 %		MINUS	3	- 2.12 %
PLUS	4	+ 1.74 %		MINUS	4	- 2.56 %
PLUS	5	+ 2.31 %		MINUS	5	- 3.01 %
PLUS	6	+ 2.88 %		MINUS	6	- 3.45 %
PLUS	7	+ 3.44 %		MINUS	7	- 3.89 %
PLUS	8	+ 4.01 %		MINUS	8	- 4.21 %
PLUS	9	+ 4.58 %		MINUS	9	- 4.41 %
PLUS	10	+ 5.15 %		MINUS	10	- 4.61 %
PLUS	11	+ 5.71 %		MINUS	11	- 4.81 %
PLUS	12	+ 6.28 %		MINUS	12	- 5.01 %
PLUS	13	+ 6.85 %		MINUS	13	- 5.08 %
PLUS	14	+ 7.42 %		MINUS	14	- 5.01 %
PLUS	15	+ 7.98 %		MINUS	15	- 4.94 %
PLUS	16	+ 8.55 %		MINUS	16	- 4.87 %
PLUS	17	+ 9.11 %		MINUS	17	- 4.80 %
PLUS	18	+ 9.67 %		MINUS	18	- 4.74 %

CHART F-15. THE PLAYER'S ADVANTAGE WITH EACH
COUNT—FOUR DECKS

When playing with four decks, and playing Las Vegas rules, the player has an advantage any time that the true count is plus one or more. As your plus count increases, your advantage increases. The minus count is very different. After the minus count goes beyond minus 13, the advantage starts reverting to the player. If the count is plus 18, the player has a big advantage (+9.67%). But, if the count is minus 18, the player does not have a big disadvantage (−4.74%).

CHART F-16. FOUR DECKS

THE PLAYER WILL HAVE LESS BLACKJACKS WITH FOUR DECKS

TOTAL CARDS	208	104	52	26	13
ACE	55.24	54.90	54.30	52.9	50.0
TEN	41.36	42.11	42.56	43.5	45.4
9	38.64	38.83	39.22	40.0	41.7
8	38.16	37.86	37.25	36.0	33.3
7	38.16	37.86	37.25	36.0	33.3
6	61.35	61.17	60.78	60.0	58.3
5	61.83	62.13	62.74	64.0	66.7
4	61.83	62.13	62.74	64.0	66.7
3	61.35	61.17	60.78	60.0	58.3
2	61.35	61.17	60.78	60.0	58.3
STIFFS	50.07	50.04	49.96	49.84	49.33
BLACKJACKS	21.0	20.9	20.7	20.3	19.5

CHART F-16. FOUR DECKS

There is little difference between playing with four decks and playing with a single deck. Your play will be more even and sure with four decks. The house has more of an advantage with four decks partly due to the fact that the player will get fewer Blackjacks. The player will get a Blackjack once in each 21 hands. With a single deck, he will get a Blackjack once in each 20.7 hands.

The dealer will get more stiffs with a 4, 5, 9, 10 up with four decks as the deck runs out. On this chart you can see why you hit more when the dealer has a seven or eight up. The dealer will not have many stiffs. A stiff is a bad hand: 3, 4, 5, 6, 12, 13, 14, 15, or 16.

CHART F-17.   THE TRUE COUNT WITH FOUR DECKS

Other books teach you to bet more, to stand more, and to double more at the last of the deck than you would at the first of the deck with the same count. But a simple schedule has never been presented before.

If you remove four fives from a complete deck, the player has an advantage of 3.04%. If there are 13 cards remaining (one of each), and you remove one five, this would have the same result. So, removing four cards from a complete deck, two cards from half a deck, or removing one card from a quarter deck, you get the same result. *You must know the amount of remaining cards in order to know your true count.* You do not need to know the exact amount of remaining cards. You only need to be able to estimate them within a quarter of a deck. *You must know the true count at all times.* Then you will know how much to bet, and how to play the hands.

You may have a running count of plus ten and have an advantage of only 2%, or you may have a running count of plus ten and have an advantage of 15% or more. You may have a running count of plus six and stand on twelve when the dealer has a three, or you may have a running count of plus six and hit when the dealer has a three. How you play each hand and how you bet your money depend upon the true count.

With four decks: if your running count were (plus or minus) twenty-four; if only a few cards had been dealt, your true count would be (plus or minus) three. If one deck were gone, your true count would be (plus or minus) four. If two decks were gone, your true count would be (plus or minus) six. If only one deck were left, your true count would be (plus or minus) twelve. If only half a deck were left, your true count would be (plus or minus) twenty-four.

CHART F-17. THE TRUE COUNT WITH FOUR DECKS

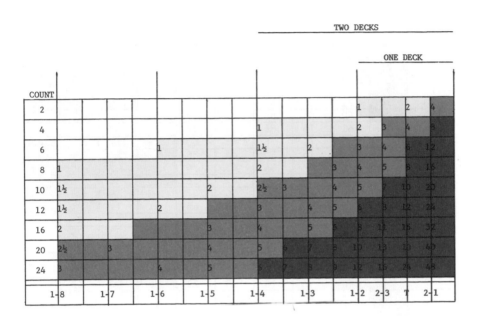

YELLOW 0.04 % OR MORE   BLUE 0.90 % OR MORE   RED 3.04 % OR MORE

TO FIND YOUR TRUE COUNT WITH FOUR DECKS, USE THE BOTTOM NUMBERS

IF 1 DECK IS GONE, DIVIDE YOUR COUNT BY 6, THIS WILL GIVE YOU THE TRUE COUNT

IF 2 DECKS ARE GONE, DIVIDE YOUR COUNT BY 4, THIS WILL GIVE YOU THE TRUE COUNT

IF 3 DECKS ARE GONE, DIVIDE YOUR COUNT BY 2, THIS WILL GIVE YOU THE TRUE COUNT

WITHOUT THE TRUE COUNT YOU COULD HAVE NO ACCURACY

YOU DETERMINE THE EXACT TRUE COUNT IN THIS MANNER:

$$\frac{26}{\text{REMAINING CARDS}} \text{ TIMES RUNNING COUNT} = \text{TRUE COUNT}$$

CHART F-18. WHEN YOU HAVE A TRUE COUNT OF PLUS TEN

	A	2	3	4	5	6	7	8	9	10
AA	55	81	92	102	108	108	80	65	51	40
22	37	0	18	34	46	35	13	26	35	42
33	42	7	12	32	41	30	25	35	43	46
66	42	8	11	27	36	21	36	41	46	46
77	53	0	10	35	39	34	10	55	63	56
88	34	21	38	49	58	58	39	6	53	56
99	1	40	54	66	76	74	57	38	7	26
XX	63	61	75	86	94	92	81	83	77	53
A2	20	5	21	36	48	40	4	12	17	25
A3	28	1	16	35	44	36	12	15	26	32
A4	31	0	17	34	43	34	13	22	30	35
A5	34	0	16	33	42	38	16	26	33	38
A6	26	10	28	44	56	47	2	19	28	33
A7	11	26	44	62	65	65	51	12	20	26
A8	24	44	64	71	80	80	70	67	25	8
A9	67	65	74	86	94	93	82	83	79	50
AX	150	150	150	150	150	150	150	150	150	150
23	39	7	3	13	20	14	23	30	40	44
24	41	8	3	12	19	14	25	36	42	46
7	36	3	7	18	25	22	5	30	40	43
8	21	8	27	47	58	55	20	4	28	34
9	3	35	55	70	81	78	55	30	3	20
10	19	68	85	96	103	101	81	66	43	14
11	28	80	93	106	109	105	73	59	45	36
12	41	18	8	0	7	2	31	37	44	44
13	51	18	6	3	7	1	42	50	50	54
14	57	18	7	2	7	2	49	52	58	59
15	57	17	6	2	7	2	49	55	60	59
16	55	17	7	2	6	5	48	54	60	59
17	39	5	4	12	14	13	8	45	50	49
18	8	17	25	29	34	40	49	10	29	29
19	27	39	44	49	54	57	69	64	23	4
WIN	35.88	26.96	37.84	47.04	52.88	49.24	26.46	15.56	2.19	15.72
BJ	39.22									9.80

This is the amount you will win or lose, in percent, when you have a true count of plus ten. This chart is provided so that you will be aware of what to expect when you have the advantage. The left column running up and down represents the player's hand. The top column running across indicates the dealer's up card. The figures in the red squares indicate the player's loss. The lighter squares indi-

CHART F-19. THE AMOUNT OF TIMES YOU WILL GET EACH HAND

	A	2	3	4	5	6	7	8	9	10
AA	48	48	48	48	48	48	48	64	64	320
22	24	5	14	14	14	14	14	19	19	96
33	24	14	5	14	14	14	14	19	19	96
66	24	14	14	14	14	5	14	19	19	96
77	24	14	14	14	14	14	5	19	19	96
88	48	29	29	29	29	29	29	19	38	192
99	48	29	29	29	29	29	29	38	19	192
XX	1520	912	912	912	912	912	912	1216	1216	5696
A2	96	48	72	72	72	72	72	96	96	480
A3	96	72	48	72	72	72	72	96	96	480
A4	96	72	72	48	72	72	72	96	96	480
A5	96	72	72	72	48	72	72	96	96	480
A6	96	72	72	72	72	48	72	96	96	480
A7	96	72	72	72	72	72	48	96	96	480
A8	128	96	96	96	96	96	96	96	128	640
A9	128	96	96	96	96	96	96	128	96	640
AX	640	480	480	480	480	480	480	640	640	3040
23	72	29	29	43	43	43	43	58	58	288
24	72	29	43	29	43	43	43	58	58	288
7	144	72	72	72	72	86	86	115	115	576
8	168	86	86	91	86	86	101	134	134	672
9	216	115	115	115	115	115	115	173	173	864
10	264	136	144	144	149	144	144	192	211	1056
11	336	182	182	187	187	187	187	250	250	1344
12	744	350	427	427	432	446	446	576	576	2880
13	744	446	350	427	427	432	432	576	576	2880
14	672	403	403	307	384	384	403	518	518	2592
15	672	403	403	403	307	384	403	518	518	2592
16	576	346	346	346	346	250	326	461	442	2208
17	608	365	365	365	365	365	269	461	461	2336
18	640	384	384	384	384	384	384	384	512	2432
19	640	384	384	384	384	384	384	512	384	2432

cate the player's gain. Example: If the player has two aces and dealer has a three, he has an advantage of 92 percent. For each dollar bet he will get back $1.92 on the average.

Chart F-19 indicates the amount of times you will get each hand in each 100,000 hands. Example: You will get two aces vs an ace 48 times in each 100,000 hands.

When the true count is plus ten the best hand for the player is eleven vs a five. The worst hand is two sevens vs a nine. Also notice that when dealer has 2-3-4-5-6, the player is better off to have 13-14-15-16 than he is to have 12. Compare this chart with Chart B-20. In Chart B-20 the count is zero.

CHART F-20.   RECORD OF 190 DAYS PLAY

When you play, many times you will play for a short while. If the table fills up, quit. If you have bad players, quit. If there are any distractions, quit. Play only under the best conditions. If playing conditions are not right, do not be in any hurry to play. You can always play tomorrow. The reason why so many players do not succeed as strategy players is that they usually come to Nevada on a week end, and they are here to play, so they will play under any condition. The best time to play is late at night, from three a.m. on.

Starting January 1, 1963, I played 190 consecutive days and kept a detailed record of the results. Many plays were for twenty minutes or less and I generally had to play for small stakes.

In the 190 days, I lost three times in a row on four occasions, and I never did lose more than three times in a row. I won 16 times in a row once, and I won 15 times in a row once. In the 190 days I lost once in each 4.3 plays.

I did not have the Advanced Point Count perfected then. Now, when I play the Advanced Point Count, I lose about one time in each nine playing sessions.

Gambling is a funny thing. A roulette wheel has about the same advantage as we have, nevertheless, it will lose about one time in each seven days on the average, with short play. If gambling did not go to extremes there would be no gambling.

Again, the systems do not work every time, just most of the time. When you lose, expect it. Never play to get even.

CHART F-20. RECORD OF 190 DAYS PLAY

W 200	W 160	L 140	W 60	W 220	W 340	W 370
W 140	W 180	W 150	W 100	W 140	W 1130	W 20
W 60	L 280	W 50	W 50	W 160	W 160	L 330
W 120	W 120	W 40	W 280	W 740	W 40	W 270
W 180	W 545	W 135	W 500	W 290	W 905	L 100
L 100	W 400	W 65	W 105	W 110	L 300	W 880
W 60	L 260	L 550	W 105	W 225	L 140	W 70
W 130	L 30	L 130	W 155	L 235	L 500	W 10
W 140	L 70	L 200	W 135	L 625	W 240	W 700
W 140	W 160	W 70	W 310	L 240	W 380	W 40
W 200	W 250	W 190	W 80	W 190	L 380	
W 390	W 200	L 60	W 200	W 40	W 1260	
W 120	W 60	W 185	W 195	W 250	W 400	
W 70	L 120	W 160	W 60	W 200	W 140	
W 120	W 20	W 40	W 180	W 35	W 135	
W 40	W 110	W 180	L 200	L 280	W 10	
L 150	W 420	W 80	W 270	W 70	W 360	
W 30	W 20	L 100	L 310	W 160	I. 440	
L 180	W 300	L 80	W 470	L 180	W 150	
W 150	W 40	W 230	L 40	W 450	W 140	
L 180	W 320	W 40	W 100	W 360	L 400	
W 130	L 40	W 200	L 40	W 140	L 140	
W 140	W 90	L 30	W 130	W 190	W 150	
W 400	W 220	W 395	W 145	W 340	W 250	
W 780	W 460	W 170	W 300	W 390	L 150	
W 790	L 150	L 170	W 210	L 170	W 90	
L 130	W 210	W 50	W 220	W 250	L 870	
L 330	L 80	W 150	W 20	W 30	W 50	
W 680	W 320	W 200	W 110	W 210	L 100	
W 830	W 190	L 120	W 60	W 320	L 250	

EACH 30 DAYS	W 24 L 6	W 22 L 8	W 20 L 10	W 26 L 4	W 24 L 6	W 19 L 11	W 8 L 2
WIN	$4970	$3765	$1200	$3960	$3780	$2660	$1930

TOTAL WIN $22,265.   AVERAGE EACH 30 DAYS $3515.54

WON 143 PLAYS   LOST 47 PLAYS

CHART F-21. PLAYING WITH A PARTNER

Whenever I play, I usually play with a girl partner. This looks more natural, and I have the advantage of seeing two hands, plus the fact, that when the pit boss sees a girl playing, he knows that she has no advantage. If you are going to play with a partner, I suggest that you teach her this chart. She will be right about 97% of the time. When an extreme situation does come up, you can always tell her to play differently. If your partner learns this chart, she can play with you whenever you play any of the count strategies.

Anything in a solid color, she must always do. Anything in red print, she plays according to the count. Example: She has 13, dealer has a 3. This is optional, she may hit or she may stand, according to the count.

THE REVERE POINT COUNT STRATEGY 143

CHART F-21. PLAYING WITH A PARTNER
Red print is optional

	2	3	4	5	6	7	8	9	10	ACE
8	H	D	D	D	D	H	H	H	H	H
9	D	D	D	D	D	D	D	H	H	H
10	D	D	D	D	D	D	D	D	D	D
11	D	D	D	D	D	D	D	D	D	D
12	H	H	H	H	H	H	H	H	H	H
13	H	H	H	H	H	H	H	H	H	H
14	H	H	H	H	H	H	H	H	H	H
15	H	H	H	H	H	H	H	H	H	H
16	S	S	S	S	S	H	H	H	H	H
A2	H	D	D	D	D	H	H	H	H	H
A3	H	D	D	D	D	H	H	H	H	H
A4	H	D	D	D	D	H	H	H	H	H
A5	H	D	D	D	D	H	H	H	H	H
A6	D	D	D	D	D	H	H	H	H	H
A7	D	D	D	D	D	S	S	H	H	H
A8	D	D	D	D	D	S	S	S	S	S
A9	S	D	D	D	D	S	S	S	S	S
AA	P	P	P	P	P	P	P	P	P	P
22	P	P	P	P	P	P	H	H	H	H
33	H	P	P	P	P	P	H	H	H	H
44	H	D	D	D	D	H	H	H	H	H
66	P	P	P	P	P	H	H	H	H	H
77	P	P	P	P	P	P	H	H	H	H
88	P	P	P	P	P	P	P	P	P	P
99	P	P	P	P	P	P	P	P	S	P
XX	S	P	P	P	P	S	S	S	S	S

CHART F-22. OPTIONAL PRACTICE CHART

HIT-STAND	DOUBLE 8-9-10-11	A2 TO A9
2-3-4-5-6 UP STAND ON 16 12 TO 15 OPTIONAL	DOUBLE ON 10-11 4-5-6 UP ALWAYS OTHERS OPTIONAL	A2 TO A6 3-4-5-6 OPTIONAL OTHERS HIT
7-8-9-X-A UP HIT 12 OR 13 14 TO 16 OPTIONAL	DOUBLE ON 9 2 TO 8 OPTIONAL OTHERS HIT	YOU HAVE A7 9 OR 10 HIT 7 OR 8 STAND
HARD 17 TO 20 ALWAYS STAND	DOUBLE ON 8 3 TO 6 OPTIONAL OTHERS HIT	A8 OR A9 3-4-5-6 OPTIONAL OTHERS STAND

CHART F-22. OPTIONAL PRACTICE CHART

Many things will not seem important to the player who is just starting to learn to play one of the strategies. I have included everything that will make learning the strategies as simple as possible. You must have a right way to do everything, including practice. Make a copy of this chart and use it to practice with Chart B-9.

PRACTICE WITH CHART B-9

You have 12 dealer has 6. Optional, you may hit or stand.
You have AA dealer has 3. You always split.
You have 14 dealer has 2. Optional, you may hit or stand.
You have 10 dealer has 9. Optional, you may hit or double.
You have 44 dealer has 6. Optional, you may hit or double.
You have 13 dealer has 8. You always hit.
You have A8 dealer has 5. Optional, you may stand or double.

THE ADVANCED
POINT COUNT STRATEGY

It is very easy to win at Blackjack; in fact, there is more money to be made playing Blackjack than can be made in most occupations and professions.

As unbelievable as it may seem, prior to the Revere strategies there has been no possible way for anyone to learn how to play Blackjack accurately and in a manner where they could play without fear of being barred. In the past, the player in search of knowledge had two choices:

1. Professor Thorp's books.

2. The systems sold by mail order.

Professor Thorp's strategies are extremely difficult to learn. He is a mathematics professor, not a professional Blackjack player. His strategies are accurate; however, we have been able to improve on his Basic Strategy.

Mail order systems are made to be sold. I know of no completely accurate mail order system. Some of the promoters make fabulous claims in their literature of winnings, but often the claims are less fact than fable. Some of the "easy to learn" mail order systems are at least as difficult to master as the Thorp strategies.

The Revere strategies are the first to be devised by someone who has been a successful Blackjack player. I do not know of any promoter of a mail order system who has been capable of winning in the casinos. They make claims of winning and even go so far as to try and get themselves barred to gain publicity. If any of the promoters had a winning system he would be foolish to sell it. If you have an accurate system and you play well, there is more money to be made playing Blackjack than there is in selling Blackjack systems. As stated elsewhere in this book, I did not release any information until I had been barred from playing in all of the Nevada casinos.

To devise a winning and playable Blackjack strategy you must be an experienced player and you must be willing to spend thousands and thousands of dollars on computer time. I do not know of any mail order system on which the promoter has spent a quarter on computer time.

Mastering the Revere Point Count Strategy will insure your being a winner almost every time you play, under almost all conditions. However, if you plan to play for serious money full-time, I suggest you learn the Advanced Point Count Strategy. With the Advanced Point Count you will have the maximum possible percentage in your favor at all times. There is no way in the world to gain another fraction of a percent on any decision or set of conditions whatsoever.

With the Advanced Point Count it is possible to play in all of the casinos in the world and have a sure advantage, even though rules in some of the foreign casinos are very unfavorable for the player. Thus, armed with this advanced strategy you can make money playing Blackjack at your leisure in countries all over the world.

Once you have mastered the Advanced Point Count, you will be able to fly around the world first class, live and play in the finest resort hotels, eat nothing but gourmet foods, and return showing a profit.

Some of the countries which have the bigger casinos include: Portugal, Spain, Greece, Turkey, Isle of Man, Italy, France, Germany, Austria, Monaco, Yugoslavia, England (300 casinos) the Scandinavian countries, South Korea, Macao, Australia, Tasmania, Noumea, Malaysia, Philippines, Singapore, Egypt, Swaziland, Tangiers, Ghana, Kenya, Bot wana, Lesotho, Iran, Nepal, Mediterranean Islands, Gibraltar, Zaire, Malta, Lebanon, Scotland, Madera, Wales, Columbia, Ecuador. Surinam, Panama, there are more than forty casinos in the West Indies area: Freeport, Nassau, Puerto Rico (12 casinos), St. Martin, Curacao, Aruba, Bonaire, San Andres, Dominican Republic and Haiti.

It is just as easy to play with four decks, and you have several advantages: the pit bosses do not watch you as closely; you can bet more freely; and four decks will not run as extreme as a single deck.

Some casinos in Las Vegas and in other parts of the world currently offer "Surrender." If you are dealt a bad hand and you don't like it, you may give up half your bet and throw your hand in. When you are keeping track of the cards, this is a big advantage. Sometimes you may save as much as thirty percent.

If you intend to play seriously and wish to insure having the maximum possible advantage under all conditions, it would be wise to consider learning the Advanced Point Count. This system cost more than $25,000 to develop, a cost which includes thousands upon thousands of man hours, and more costly computer time than has been expended on any other system in the world.

In this system, each card is given a value, plus or minus, in proportion to the exact effect it has upon the remaining cards when it is removed from the deck. The card values were obtained by computer by Julian Braun. This is the first time the accurate card values have been published. Dr. Thorp gave the card values when four cards of a kind were removed from the deck and a special strategy was played.

With this advanced strategy, you do not have to vary the size of your bets. If you play in Las Vegas with a single deck you can win with a flat bet, which means you bet the same amount at all times. With a flat bet you have an advantage of 3.2%. However, I do suggest that you vary your bets from one to two units. This will increase your advantage to 4.2%.

The Advanced Point Count Strategy is not difficult to learn. After you have learned the Revere Point Count Strategy, you can learn the Advanced Point Count in a few days. After you have learned and perfected it, you will find that it will be easy to play.

You will know your advantage at all times, allowing you to make bets in direct proportion to the advantage you have. When you play the Advanced Point Count, if you bet $5 units and bet in the manner I suggest, you will win $45 to $50 an hour on the average.

I intend to make the Advanced Point Count available to the public in my next book. I do not plan to publish this book in the near future. However, I have received many requests concerning this strategy.

To solve this problem and provide a service to those of you who are interested in obtaining this strategy immediately, I will send it to you by mail. You will receive this strategy before it is published in book form.

For optimum results there are two Advanced Point Count Strategies available. One strategy is superior for playing with one deck and the other strategy is superior for playing with multiple decks.

With either of these strategies you receive a complete playing strategy for ANY possible hand you may get when playing with one, two, or four decks. Also, a playing strategy that will enable you to play in any casino in the world; double after splits, and how to play when the dealer does not take a Hole Card. (Blackjack is played this way in all of the foreign casinos). Surrender figures are included, plus an entirely different way to bet your money that is easier and more accurate. Betting your money accurately is the most important part ur of the game, especially with four decks.

With these strategies you will make many strange plays. There is an exact way to play every hand. Some of the unusual plays are: double down on A7 vs 7; A8 vs 7; A9 vs 7; A9 vs 8; split two tens vs 7 or 8. Sometimes you may stand on 13 vs 7, at another time you may hit 17.

These strategies will be in a twenty four page book and will include practice charts, and will point out to you the correct way to learn. The price for either of these strategies and all the above information is $200. If you intend to play exclusively with one deck you need the strategy devised for one deck play. If you intend to play with multiple decks you need the strategy devised for multiple decks. If you should decide to purchase either strategy, please specify which strategy you would like.

I guarantee either strategy to be superior to any other strategy that has ever been available to Blackjack players.

I also have a four or more deck playing strategy for the Revere Point Count Strategy. There are forty-eight changes from the one deck playing strategy. If you send for this four deck strategy, you will also receive surrender figures for one and four or more decks.

The Plus-Minus count is a winning count, and it is easy to play. The playing strategy is only an approximate playing strategy for one deck. I have an accurate playing strategy for the Plus-Minus count that you may play with one, two, or four or more decks. If you plan to play seriously, you should definitely have this strategy — then you can play and win with a full table. Surrender figures and an accurate betting strategy you can use in any casino in the world are included with this strategy. Atlantic City information is also included.

The price for the four deck Point Count Strategy, or the accurate playing strategy for the Plus-Minus Strategy is $25.00.

Personal consultation is available.

Lawrence Revere Ltd.

1517 Rexford Place

Las Vegas, Nevada 89104

Phone: (702) 385-1585

Chapter 11
OTHER BLACKJACK SYSTEMS

Every day I get many letters and phone calls from Blackjack players wanting information. The two questions asked most frequently are: "If I learn a count strategy, how long will I be able to play before I am barred?" and, "How accurate are the other systems sold by mail; do they really win as the authors claim?"

The answer to the first question is straightforward: if the bosses in any casino think you have an advantage over the house they will bar you from playing. It's as simple as that. They consider losing house money a serious matter.

The solution to the problem is; never let the casino bosses know that you have an advantage. This is relatively easy, and if you follow the playing rules I suggest, you will never be barred from playing.

There are thirty casinos in Las Vegas and each has three shifts. Therefore, there are in effect ninety "different" places to play without ever seeing the same casino personnel twice. If you never play on any one shift more than an hour at a time, it is virtually impossible for you to be detected as a card counter.

I played in all of the Nevada casinos for many years before I was barred. The reason that I was barred was that years back we did not have the accuracy made possible by today's computers. As a result, we had to vary the size of our bets to such an extreme that we did not look at all like average players.

The most important thing is to have an accurate system so that you do not have to vary the size of your bets appreciably in order to win. I suggest you bet one or two units and sometimes you parlay your money. That way your betting manner looks like everyone else's. I suggest you play exclusively with one and two decks when playing in Nevada.

Very few players have been barred from playing in all of the casinos. In looking through the books the casinos keep on people who are restricted from playing, I found there were only seven of us who were barred from playing in all of the Nevada casinos because we were card counters. The books have about 300 names and pictures, supplied by the state gaming agency and by detective agencies. Most of the people in the books were barred strictly for cheating, not for being detected as card counters.

After many years of working with students interested in winning at Blackjack, I have noticed most are puzzled by one seemingly perplexing question. As one man expressed it, "If beating a Blackjack game is as easy as you say, why aren't the casinos flooded with professional players, and why do the casinos continue to win more money every year?"

The question is legitimate, for it has been proven countless times that 21 games can be beaten by people who have a command of a proper playing system. So, why do the casinos continue to rake in millions of dollars over the 21 tables? The real answer is two-fold.

First, I should define what I mean by "easy" when I say that Blackjack games are easy to beat. The "easy" I speak of does not mean that someone can spend a total of ten minutes memorizing a "magic" set of numbers or fasten a charmed amulet around his neck. That might be easy, all right, but it will do nothing to alter the house percentage in the long run.

The kind of "easy" I refer to means simply that once a person has trained himself in the use of a proper system and is adroit with it he will win nine times out of ten. He will do this at his convenience, at a casino of his choosing, and he will take home whatever amount of money he feels he can take without causing undue suspicion.

His win rate will average $50, or $100 or $500 or more an hour, depending upon how much money he has to wager and how well he plays the game. He will be spending his time in pleasant surroundings and he will expend no more energy than a secretary or a file clerk. In this sense, beating a 21 game is "easy".

Unfortunately, most people like to think of the rewards without thinking of the work, even when the work really doesn't amount to much. And when it comes to 21, it's absolutely essential to put in the necessary time to learn a system with which there is no gamble.

In the front of the book (How to Get the Most Out of This Book) the number of hours required to master the various strategies is carefully spelled out. If you spend the required amount of hours to master this material, you will be among the few really capable of beating Blackjack consistently. Don't forget, though, the hours listed are only averages. Mastery of the material is the important thing whether it takes you more or less time.

But, there's a second part to the answer of why casinos aren't flooded with people beating their Blackjack games. The fact is that many people have spent unlimited time and study in trying to learn to beat a Blackjack game, but have spent that time on a totally worthless system, or one capable of yielding a low return. This is why casinos love Blackjack system players. Either the players have not done the proper amount of work to make a good system work for them, or they have done a great deal of work with a system which is incapable of winning.

It is a fact of life that if a casino boss thinks you really have a true edge at Blackjack he will bar you from playing. But, casino bosses also know that everyone who plays Blackjack *thinks* he has some edge, some gimmick, or some betting strategy which will enable him to win. That is why people play Blackjack, because they think they can beat the game. But if all the system or strategy players were barred from all the Blackjack games in all the casinos in Nevada there would probably be only enough action for two tables in the state, one each in Las Vegas and Reno, reserved for hot hunch players.

So the reason the casinos still make money despite the proven fact that Blackjack *can* be beaten is because not enough people are capable of beating them, due to either lack of work or a poor strategy.

Let's assume you are interested enough in winning at Blackjack to spend enough hours practicing to become proficient at the system you choose. That's the first requirement and that only leaves the strategy which you are going to concentrate upon. Which is best? Which of all the systems offered through the mail or in books will give you the greatest advantage?

First, take the mail order systems. People who have purchased mail order systems at any price, have actually ended up losing much more money than they otherwise would have, due to the fact that most of these "systems" are strictly junk. They literally are not worth the paper they are written on, yet some of their authors make fabulous claims and have the audacity to charge as much as an average week's wages for them. I do not know of one person who has bought a mail order system and has been able to win with it.

Just imagine the number of people who have paid good money for this kind of bad information, spent many hours practicing, then traveled perhaps across country to play in Nevada casinos only to lose. This is not only unfortunate but as was noted before, a major part of the reason the clubs aren't afraid of most strategy players.

The fact is, most Blackjack systems I have analyzed are either so inaccurate that they are not worth the space to comment upon, or only accurate enough to have won twenty years ago and not enough to make them worth learning today. In addition, some of these systems are so complex that it takes days to carefully separate their elements and analyze them. Having done that, I all too often discovered that the complexity was apparently designed by their authors in the belief that the average person would never be able to figure out why the systems should work, and would buy on faith. On the other hand, some systems are so simple that they can be proved unworkable in a few minutes. They must have been designed for the simple-minded, who believe a magic number or something of the sort will enable them to win if they pay a high enough price for it.

It has cost more than $40,000 to devise the Revere strategies. They are completely accurate. We made calculations with high speed computers using the theory of mathematical probabilities which has given us the equivalent of 9,000,000,000 hands of actually played Blackjack to devise the strategies. As an example: Julian Braun played 7,000,000 hands on computers to determine what you do with two fours when the dealer has 3-4-5-6. He discovered if the rules would not let you double down on eight, you could never split two fours when the dealer has a six, regardless of what the count may be. It is possible to split two fours when the dealer has 3-4-5 if the count is extremely high. When the rules do allow you to double down after you have split a pair, you may split two fours when dealer has 4-5-6 .

Before making some specific comments on individual systems available through the mail or in books today, let me make one unequivocal statement. There is no Blackjack system available by mail or in books at any price which is as accurate as the Revere Point Count Strategy presented in this book. I will be happy to prove this statement by computer or by actual play anytime the rewards are such to justify my time. But please note carefully what I have said. In other words, the Point Count Strategy you have purchased in **this book is far more superior in accuracy to any other system avail-**able on the market today.

Note also what I have left out. I did not say that the Point Count Strategy in this book gives the maximum possible yield when playing Blackjack. The maximum yield is available only to those playing the Revere Advanced Point Count Strategy, discussed in the previous chapter. However, you can buy no other Blackjack system through the mails or in books superior to the Point Count Strategy.

After reading this book, and the material with the promises the mail order promoters send out, how can you tell who knows more and which system is ultimately superior?

In an attempt to answer this kind of question, and to prove once and for all exactly which is the most powerful strategy, I issue the following challenge:

I will be happy to put up $10,000 against an equal amount to play against any author, disseminator or promoter of any Blackjack system. We will agree on time and place and the conditions of play. With an equal betting spread, whoever wins the most money at the end of eight hours play with whatever system he chooses to use will take the money.

Now, a few words about other specific systems: in 1961, Professor Edward O. Thorp wrote the book "Beat the Dealer." This was the first Blackjack book to present an accurate winning Blackjack strategy. The Ten Count Strategy appeared here for the first time. This system is still superior to all of the systems sold by mail order or in other books. In the ten count systems you have to vary the size of your bets in order to win. The casinos are alert for players who change the size of their bets, so this strategy is practically obsolete.

In 1966, Dr. Thorp revised his book. The Complete Point Count appeared in this edition. This is the most accurate strategy available today with the exception of the Revere strategies. The count in the Revere strategies is superior. Dr. Thorp's count was: 2-3-4-5-6 counted plus one; 7-8-9 counted zero; and aces and tens counted minus one as they were removed from the deck. This was a very good count but it was almost impossible for a new player to learn the playing strategy. You had to keep an exact count of the remaining cards, then form an index to play the hands.

Despite the complexity of the Thorp strategies, they were accurate. They are still used as a base by many authors of other Blackjack books and systems. Though many have succeeded in simplifying Dr. Thorp's systems, it has always been at the expense of accuracy.

In 1965, Dr. Allan Wilson authored an excellent book, "The Casino Gambler's Guide", published by Harper & Row. This book covered all of the casino games, and in addition, presented new material on the subject of betting systems and money management. His coverage of 21 alone had two-thirds as many pages as Dr. Thorp's book, which dealt exclusively with Blackjack. Wilson introduced his own simple point count system, which dated back to the mid-1950's, when scientific analysis of Blackjack was just getting under way. He readily admitted in his own book, however, that the Thorp 10-count was superior to his own Wilson count. Over the years, Wilson has examined many point count systems, and he enthusiastically endorses the Revere Point Count Strategy as the most powerful of all of the Blackjack strategies.

Although Wilson's treatment of count systems in the present edition of his book is getting obsolete, there is much in his coverage of other topics on Blackjack to make it required reading for any serious player. To mention just a few specific items: (1) he gives a complete sample calculation for a typical Blackjack hand, showing why it is far better to hit than to stand on 10-6 versus a dealer 7; (2) he describes the use of computers to simulate Blackjack play; (3) He shows step by step how favorable insurance situations can build up as you approach the end of the deck, and (4) he compares the merits of numerous books and magazine articles regarding the quality of their coverage of Blackjack.

Wilson's four-chapter coverage of roulette is the best in existence, superior even to several books which cover only the game of roulette. It contains a detailed discussion and long-term records on "biased" (i.e. mechanically imperfect) roulette wheels, a subject hardly ever mentioned by any other author, let alone presented in any detail. His book was the first to show correctly how to calculate the odds at baccarat, and is one of the few books to demonstrate the crushing house percentage on keno.

But, it is in the area of betting systems that the "Casino Gambler's Guide" is probably most unique. His exposition of the common misconceptions about the law of averages, and his analysis of various intricate betting schemes, are excellent.

A computer programmer in the aerospace industry, Dr. Wilson formerly taught college physics. One might expect his book to be tough reading but surprisingly, he combines a convincing precision for the mathematically trained reader with a clarity of writing for the layman. It is much easier to follow than many of the muddled and inconsistent products cranked out by hacks who don't really know what they are talking about. A reading of this fine book is truly a must for every intelligent gambler.

A new mail order system priced at $20.00 is published by David Skovand. Rouge et Noir publishes a monthly newsletter for gamblers. In a recent issue, they wrote a review of the Skovand system. It stated: "Blackjack — Single Column System — published by David C. Skovand — 12 pages. The system is advertised as a card count system which tells how many large cards remain in the deck, and how many small cards remain at any time.

"In the normal point count system the number of high cards is subtracted from the number of small cards so that only the difference is available. The point count indicated the amount of excess of either low cards (negative count) or high cards (positive count).

"Skovand has the interesting concept of evaluating a high card as +100 and the small cards as +1 in his system 1. When a high card is seen you add 100 to the count; when a low card is seen you add 1.

The count at any time tells you how many high cards and low cards have been seen. The information then lets you easily determine how many low and high cards remain. The player then has both a point count, and a method of determining the ratio of non tens to tens. A sophisticated player can then use the point count strategy when it best applies and the ten count strategy when it is more effective.

"Unfortunately, Skovand does not utilize the full information that is available from his unique counting system.

"The author does not neutralize the 8 in his system; instead he neutralizes the 9 and the Ace. Neutralizing (not counting) the nine is acceptable, but neutralizing the Ace is ridiculous. Skovand's logic is that if the 8 is neutralized and then bunches up at the end of the deck when the ten count is high, the appearance of an 8 can hurt the player who is expecting a ten value card. Skovand then deduces that if the nine and ace are neutralized they cannot hurt the player when they bunch up at the end of a deck with a high ten value count.

"But the count is supposed to reflect the deck value, and ignoring the ace distorts the deck value for the entire deck. Introducing this gross error to compensate for a phenomenon that occurs infrequently doesn't help the user of the system. The good Blackjack systems work because they give proper attention to the basic card values. Approximations for the purpose of simplification are often acceptable, but ignoring the most important card in the deck doesn't make for an acceptable Blackjack system.

"Skovand's betting plan also leaves much to be desired. The author recommends a 1 unit low bet, a 3 unit medium bet, and a 10 unit bet for situations favoring the player. For unusually favorable situations the system recommends a 15 unit bet. A 1-3-10-15 betting sequence will cause many dealers to shuffle up the favorable deck situations. (You could only bet in this manner if you were playing at home.)

"The strategy indicates a change in playing strategy for the different bet sizes. But the bet size is really a measure of the ratio of tens to non tens, and the strategy is adjusted to reflect the count.

"In Skovand's Single Column System 2, the 4 and 5 are given twice the weight of the other low cards. This is not as accurate a count as in System 1.

"Blackjack — Single Column System has the germ of a good idea. But the unique counting system is not exploited properly. We do not recommend the purchase of the system."

Another Blackjack system is sold by W. B. McGhee of Las Vegas. It is a Plus-Minus system. His count is, A-2-3-4-5-6 count plus one. 8-9-10 count minus one. The price is $50.00

The system offered by Rouge et Noir is $40 and includes a one year subscription to the newsletter. In this system, you count 2-3-4-5-6 plus one, 7-8-9 count zero, and aces and tens count minus one as they are removed from the deck. They have modified Professor Thorp's very good Point Count Strategy, which was difficult to learn, and made it into an accurate and playable system. This I suggest is a good buy.

Charles Crayne has a system for sale entitled "Blackjack is my Business", which sells for $20. This is not a Blackjack system; instead it is a betting system. It is an unfortunate fact that no betting system ever devised can overcome the house advantage.

Most amateur gamblers are confused as to how to bet their money. Most of them assume that if they had some magic way of betting they could come to Las Vegas and become wealthy. There is no magic way to bet your money. When you are playing in the casinos where the house has the advantage, you are better off to bet the same amount at all times. This probably sounds foolish to most players; it would have seemed foolish to me years ago.

The way most players want to bet, and what seems like the most logical way is: bet small when you are unlucky and you are losing bets, and bet more when you are lucky and you are winning bets. Example: bet $5; if you win, bet $10; if you win, bet $20; if you win that bet, you have $40. That is a great way to bet, *when you win.* If this betting method were to succeed there would be no casinos in Nevada, because this is the way most gamblers generally play. The odds are seven to one against winning three bets in a row. So, once in eight times you will win three bets in a row if you have an even gamble. (When playing in the casinos where the house has the advantage, you will not win three bets in a row once in eight times.)

If someone were tossing a coin, and you were to play a betting progression system where you progressed when you lost, 2-4-8, etc., at the end of one million bets you would break even. Your betting method would not benefit you in any way. If you were to play a progression system where you progressed when you won, 2-4-8, etc., at the end of one million bets you would break even. The betting system would not help you in any way. If you were to play a Crayne-type system you would get the same results.

The only way you can have an advantage in the casino is when you are playing Blackjack and you are keeping track of the cards. Then you bet differently. You make small bets when the house has the advantage, and you make larger bets when you have the advantage.

Allan Wilson covers betting systems in Chapter 16. The following material is from his book:

"1. This chapter reveals the extensive mathematical analysis of the double up and other progressions that I have made, as well as penetrating analyses of other betting systems.

"2. I have read a vast amount of literature on the subject of gambling, as the references list indicates. In *none* of this literature have I ever *read* a verifiable account of a successful betting system.

"3. In a period exceeding ten years, I have spent an accumulated time of many months in the casinos of Reno and Las Vegas, and I have never *seen* a successful betting system in action, nor have I ever *heard* of a successful betting system.

"4. I have a personal knowledge of several individualists who have spent *years* of their lives experimenting with systems, and these persons have done nothing but lose huge amounts of money.

"5. So many million people have devoted so much time over the years, both in this country and abroad, to devise successful betting systems, that it seems extremely unlikely that nobody would have stumbled onto at least one such system if any existed.

"If you think you have a winning system, if you are a sceptic, if you think you have a system, do yourself the following favor. Play your system on paper for a length of time sufficient to double your bankroll several times. Double it three times, so that you have eight times what you started with. Don't settle for winning 20 percent or 50 percent of your bankroll, or even doubling it just once. Double it three times. Give it the acid test. Get into the long run with it. My definition of the long run for testing a system is the length of time sufficient to double your investment three times.

(Most system players who do make a trial run on paper make the mistake of too short a test!) For your test run on paper, you might do well to use the random number table in Appendix F.

"If you succeed in doubling three times without going broke, try to do it again, and if that succeeds too, write me and I shall publish it in the next edition of this book as the rarest event of the twentieth century."

In a review of the Charley Crayne system, Rouge et Noir stated the following:

"This widely advertised system is not a card counting procedure; it is a betting system instead.

"Crayne uses a betting progression of 1, 1, 1, 1, 1, 2, 2, 2, 2, 2, 5, 5, 5, 5, 5. If you win your first bet, you start the series over since the objective of the progression is to win 1 unit. If you lose, you make the next bet called for in the progression. When you win, after previously losing, you let the previous bet and win ride and add the next bet as well. When you win two bets in a row, you revert back to the point in the progression dictated in your cash position. Should the double win result in a win for the series, you would start over. If you win back everything but the first unit, you would start with the second bet of the progression. If you have a net loss of 2 units for the progression, you move back to the third bet in the progression, etc. You then pick up the strategy dictated by the revised position in the progression.

"The Crayne gimmick is that he describes the 1, 1, 1, 1, 1, 2, 2, 2, 2, 2, 5, 5, 5, 5, 5 progression as three banks. The first bank is composed of the five 1 unit bets; the second bank consists of the five 2 unit bets; and the third bank consists of the five 5 unit bets. The three banks (stacks of chips) are used to help identify the position in the series. Any excess chips are removed from the table as each progression is started anew.

"Anyone with a reasonable background in mathematics knows that you can't change a house advantage game into one with a player advantage through the use of a betting system. And with the Blackjack strategy suggested by Crayne, the house has a decided advantage over the player.

"Why do Crayne type systems sell? A player using the progression risks 40 units to win 1 unit. In an even game he would be expected to win 40 units, on the average, for each case of a loss of the entire 40 unit stake. With the Crayne Blackjack strategy the player, on the average, can be expected to win 39 units against the loss of a 40-unit stake.

"Since averages apply rigorously only to a large number of bets, some players using the Crayne system are lucky and get by without a catastrophic loss. Unlucky players are wiped out without ever achieving any significant win. The lucky players swear by the Crayne system, while the unlucky players swear at such systems.

"Crayne makes the ridiculous statement on page 15 of his book that you will never quit a loser over a stretched-out period of time if you stick right to the Charlie Crayne 15 Play System with Money Management. This is nonsense. Crayne himself hedges on the same page; apparently part of the system is to knock off playing when you reach the desired objective in a period less than estimated.

"The system also requires that you recognize when cards cycle against you. On page 41 Crayne suggests, "Don't sit there and challenge the dealer and just get your brains beat out . . . " All of a sudden the foolproof mathematical progression requires that you have some psychic ability. But if you have some psychic ability why limit your wins by the Crane progression, why not take advantage of such ability to win big?

"Crayne's book also purports to cover roulette, dice and horse racing. The most charitable thing we can say about Crayne's limited treatment of these subjects is that these also are not fields in which the author is an expert.

"We recommend strongly against the purchase of 'Blackjack Is My Business' by Charley Crayne."

There is one big advantage in playing a Crayne type system. You will never be barred from playing. Any Nevada casino will gladly pay your expenses to come here if you will play a betting progression system.

One of the most highly advertised mail order systems available today is the Goldberg Computer System, which baits the unsuspecting gambler with free information then proceeds to ask $100 for an out of date, inaccurate strategy. Many people go for it, as the literature is graphically pleasing and well written.

Unfortunately, the Goldberg ten-count is not only obsolete but it is also coupled to a betting strategy which by today's standards is foolhardy. You are told to play the hands according to how much money you have to bet. For instance, you are advised to stand on 16 vs a ten if you have bet 2 units and you are told to stand on 15 vs a ten if you have bet 4 units. You are also to take insurance if you have made a two-unit bet. Allowing bets to determine your playing strategy is a great deal like using birth control devices according to how pregnant your wife is. $100? The Ten Count Strategy in Profes-

sor Thorp's book is far superior and you can purchase the book for
$1.95!! The Goldberg system is not as accurate as the Revere Ten
Count Strategy in this book. $100? In my opinion, you would have to
have the nerve of a sky diver to ask anyone to spend $100 for a
strategy of this type.

Goldberg makes claims that he has been barred from Las Vegas
casinos because of the brilliance of his system. A recent example
will shed some light on these claims.

Goldberg went to the International Hotel with a reporter in tow.
He sat at a Blackjack table and made small bets until the deck was
very rich in large cards. Then he would make an unusually large bet.
Of course the dealer shuffled the cards. Finally, he became so much
of a bother he was asked to leave. He then made a scene and asked
the casino boss in loud tones so the reporter could verify, "Do you
mean you are barring me because I play so successfully?"

They sent a press release about the incident to the Las Vegas
newspapers. The papers checked with the hotel and got the facts,
and did not publish the story. The papers are wise to the ways of
promotion. Undoubtedly, this "evidence" of the strength of the Goldberg Computer system will be printed in some other newspapers,
and will appear in future advertisements.

Rouge et Noir gave their opinion of the Goldberg Computer System. They stated: "Goldberg is a newcomer to the mail order scene.
He advertises free information and instead issues a pitch for a high
priced system.

"The Goldberg system is a ten count strategy which in our opinion
does not reflect the latest developments in the field. But, the real
problem is with the betting strategy. Amazingly, the player is told

to play the hands according to the amount of the wager. On a straight mathematical basis the probability of winning is in no way influenced by the amount of the bet.

"We do not recommend purchase of the Goldberg system."

One of the most popular as well as one of the higher priced systems available is the Reppert system (also $100).

The Reppert Blackjack System is especially abominable. It has been promoted extensively and widely sold to misguided purchasers who paid good money for bad information. I find it simply unfortunate that Reppert should disseminate and sell information from so thin a vein of knowledge. When people pay a high price for information they should be able to expect more than they get with this system. A few facts about some particulars should explain why the Reppert system is a poor investment.

The Reppert system is a plus-minus strategy. With this system you count 2, 3, 4, 6, 7 as plus one; fives count plus two; nines and tens count minus one, and aces count minus two as they are removed from the deck. This count is either inane or insane, depending on whether you're trying to analyze it or win with it. First, he gives a five twice the value of the other small cards, a value unsupportable by math or computer. He gives a nine the same value as a ten when the nine actually has only a third the value of a ten. He gives an ace twice the value of a ten when they should have almost equal value.

The card values in the Reppert system are so distorted that even the Plus-Minus Strategy in Dr. Thorp's book is superior.

When compared to the Revere Point Count Strategy, the Reppert system completely falls apart. The Reppert card values are 48.8% more inaccurate.

There are other basic flaws in the Reppert system, notably in the lack of provision for a true count. Without a true count there is no possibility for consistency, accuracy, or predictability.

Furthermore, the system calls for a variance in betting of from one to seven units. This kind of betting spread would get an archangel barred, no matter how innocent his playing may appear. You could not play an hour in any Nevada casino without being barred.

A statement which appears in Reppert system advertising should be commented upon if only for its blatant effrontery. As a final arrogant insult, it says, "The Reppert Strategy is faster, easier, less subject to error and has a mathematically proven and certified yield that is superior to all others." The brilliance of this remark is in the implied fact that someone has found some systems which are *worse* than the Reppert System.

1. The Reppert system is not faster. It is a very hard system to play and is practically impossible for a new player to learn.

2. It is not less subject to error. There is no accuracy in the system. The count is the least accurate of any count that I have analyzed. There is no accuracy in the betting. There is no true count. Without a true count you can have no accuracy in the betting or in the play of the hands.

3. Instead of it being superior to all other systems, and having a mathematically proven and certified yield, it is the least accurate of all of the popular systems.

4. He states that his system is superior to Dr. Thorp's strategies. This is ridiculous. All of Dr. Thorp's strategies have a good count and a good playing strategy.

A new Blackjack system came out just before press time. *Systems Research* ($25), Stanford, California. Their advertising states: "The simplest, most effective Blackjack system ever devised, a strategy that can make you rich beyond your wildest dreams." They further state that the strategy can be learned in two hours.

The strategy is a plus-minus strategy, 2-3-4-5-6-7 count plus one, 9-10-Ace count minus one as they are removed from the deck. This count is 5% more inaccurate than the plus-minus count in *this* book. The Basic Strategy that they suggest is very inaccurate. The playing strategy for the count strategy is very bad. They have no provision for a true count. The only betting strategy they suggest is: "When the deck gets ten rich get out your big bets."

This strategy will win. In fact, it is better than the Goldberg system. The only thing objectionable is the false advertising. This system is far more difficult to learn than the Plus-Minus Strategy in this book, and I estimate it will take the average player three days to learn this strategy. Two hours, then become wealthy??

Though the challenge I made previously was intended for any and all takers, I would especially like to direct the attention of both Goldberg and Reppert to it, since these two system sellers tout their systems so highly in advertising as being the greatest systems available to beat the game of Blackjack.

These two are obviously not Blackjack players. If Reppert could play and were sincere about being able to beat the Blackjack games, I doubt he would continue to include his picture with the literature he sends out. If Goldberg were sincere about playing he would not advise players to act on their hands according to the size of their bets. Since they are not players of Blackjack, but rather sellers of Blackjack systems using insupportable claims in their advertising, it would be a great pleasure to take their money.

Any Ten Count is practically worthless for casino play. Anytime you give all cards ace through nine the same value, you have no accuracy.

Another system I cannot recommend is the "Carter RPI System of playing Blackjack," but the promoter is strong. His literature states: "The Carter RPI System is better than any other method because:

1. "You will win under ANY conditions. You won't make mistakes no matter how many players are at the table."
2. "Even the smartest casino operators won't stop you from playing because they won't know what you are doing."
3. "You don't need to count cards."
4. "You need very little capital. Even basic units of $1 will net you as much as $200 a day or more everytime you play."

"The DHM" is another new system. It does not deserve much comment. Their promotion states:

1. "The System is specifically designed for four decks."
2. "The only system on the market so designed."
3. "This System is unsurpassed."
4. "We do not guarantee constant winning."

This system is similar to the HI-OPT system. You count 2-3-4-5 vs tens. I found the DHM System to be worthless for four deck play.

The Basic Strategy they suggest is inaccurate, and they give only an approximate playing strategy. They give no True Count nor suggest a separate count of aces.

"The HI-OPT" has been the most talked about system in 1975. The system was highly advertised in Gamblers Quarterly. Their publicity states:

1. "The Simplest and Most Powerful Blackjack Strategy Devised to Date certified by Julian Braun B. Sc., and Lance Humble B.A., M.A., Ph.D."
2. "Professor Humble has a challenge to play Blackjack against anyone for any amount up to $50,000."
3. "Will enable you to play as well as any expert."
4. "Widespread use of the HI-OPT will cause the casinos to change the rules."
5. "Limit the sales to 300."
6. "Easy to learn, simple to use, and extremely powerful."
7. "Will show a more rapid rate of profit than any other system."
8. "12 years of computer testing by Mr. G."

They ask $200 for the system.

On April 10, 1974 Julian Braun wrote and asked me to send him the 3-4-5-6 vs tens strategy. He did not tell me he was going to sell it, therefore I sent it to him at no cost. He revised some of the figures, made the True Count much more complicated and included doubling down sometimes on 5-6-7, hitting A7 vs 2 through 8, and hitting hard 17 even when the dealer has a small card. These additions are stupid and would get the player barred from playing, and quickly. Imagine what would happen if you were to draw to hard 17 and the dealer had a 5 or 6, and you were unlucky enough to draw a 3 or 4. Julian has never played Blackjack professionally so he did not know any better. He sold the system to Lance Humble who has taken lessons from me and I do not consider him to be a Blackjack authority.

With the HI-OPT strategy, you count 3-4-5-6 vs tens. This system was first used by a group of Las Vegas Blackjack players in 1963. I devised it with an accurate playing strategy early in 1968, and I discarded it in 1969. It would not win as much as the Plus-Minus strategy.

Charles Einstein also devised the system in 1968 and included it in his book "How to Win at Blackjack," but he devised the playing strategy by guess. He did not use a computer. He came to my house in 1968 and I told him if he had phoned I would have given him an accurate playing strategy. I showed him my figures and pointed out errors in his book.

You can devise a strategy that is simple or one that is very complicated. The more complicated the strategy (higher count), generally the more accuracy you have. You must play a count that you can play accurately. The most important thing is accuracy in what you are playing. If you play Basic Strategy and you are playing on the Las Vegas Strip and play perfectly you will break even. If you keep track of fours, bet more and less and do it accurately you will win. If you play a Ten Count strategy you will win a little more. If you play the DHM or the HI-OPT you will win more. If you play the simple Plus-Minus Strategy with an accurate playing strategy you will win more than any of the previous strategies mentioned. If you want more accuracy you can play the Revere Point Count or one of the Revere advanced counts.

In the literature mailed out for the HI-OPT system they challeng-
ed anyone to play for $50,000. I answered their letter, I told them I
was ready to play and I could get them ten other players. They did
not answer my letter.

On December 28, 1974 Julian Braun wrote me a letter stating he
had no part in the publicity or the false advertising regarding the
HI-OPT system. All of the publicity was done by Mr. Humble and
was not the fault of Julian Braun.

I like to believe everything I read in print, but you cannot believe
what you read about the Mail Order systems. They have to make
fabulous claims to get buyers. There has never been a Mail Order
system offered for sale that is as accurate or as powerful as the Revere Point Count in my book. I do not make false claims. If I write
something you can bet on it.

When playing Blackjack you need all of the accuracy you can
handle, especially when playing with four decks. When playing with
four decks, the most important part is betting your money accurately. I have found the Ten Count, the DHM and the HI-OPT systems to be practically worthless for four deck play. Example: when
playing the HI-OPT system, you count the two, seven, eight, nine
and ace as zero. When playing you never have balanced distribution.
You will always have a surplus or shortage of these cards, and in
that way you are betting your money inaccurately a large part of
the time.

To devise a Blackjack strategy, there are two requirements that
are a must:

1. You must know how much advantage or disadvantage each
card gives the player, and you must know the advantage or disad-

vantage each card gives the dealer in the play of the hands.

2.   You must be a skilled player with many years experience at the tables.

I have played the game successfully for more than 20 years. I do not know of another writer or system seller who has played the game for two months successfully.

I have had many people come to my home who have bought one of the Mail Order systems. I do not know of one person that has made money with them. Many were poor people who could not afford to waste the money. They bought the systems because of the false advertising.

If you have bought one of the many worthless systems through the mail, and if you bought it because of the false advertising, if you will return the system to them, they will refund your money.

Even though I am barred from playing in the Nevada casinos, Blackjack is still my business, Las Vegas is still my home. I spend half of each year playing Blackjack in the foreign casinos. The past three years I have traveled all over Africa, 7 trips to the West Indies, 6 trips to London, 4 trips to France, 3 trips to Canada, 2 trips to Iowa, three trips to South Korea and Macao, trips to Portugal, Italy, Monte Carlo, Yugoslavia, Austria, Greece, Germany and Australia. The rest of my time I spend teaching and refining my strategies with the latest developments in computer technology.

I enjoy helping people. If you have any questions please write or phone. I will be happy to help you.

If you send your name and address, I will keep you informed of any new changes, junket information and playing conditions in the foreign casinos. If you have any questions, please send a stamped self-addressed envelope.

Each card has a value for the player or for the house

HI-OPT PRICE $200	CARD	TRUE VALUE	COUNT	ERROR
	2	0.53	0	66 %
With this system you have	3	0.61	+1	49
a count of +4 and -4	4	0.81	+1	24
	5	1.03	+1	4
You should count the four	6	0.61	+1	49
as +0.81	7	0.40	0	50
	8	0.00	0	0
When you count +1 you are	9	-0.26	0	32
in error 23.75 % compared	X	-0.72	-1	35 (4)
to the other counts	A	-0.85	0	106

Average Percent of error each card 39.69 %

HI-OPT-TWO PRICE $200	CARD	TRUE VALUE	COUNT	ERROR
	2	1.06	+1	4 %
With this system you have	3	1.23	+1	14
a count of +8 and -8	4	1.62	+2	24
	5	2.07	+2	4
You should count the four	6	1.23	+1	14
as +1.62	7	0.80	+1	12
	8	0.00	0	0
When you count +2 you are	9	-0.52	0	32
in error 23.75 % compared	X	-1.44	-2	35 (4)
to the other counts	A	-1.70	0	106

Average Percent of error each card 26.92 %

SIMPLE PLUS-MINUS $9.95	CARD	TRUE VALUE	COUNT	ERROR
	2	0.66	+1	34 %
With this system you have	3	0.77	+1	23
a count of +5 and -5	4	1.01	+1	1
	5	1.29	+1	29
You should count the four	6	0.77	+1	23
as +1.01	7	0.50	0	50
	8	0.00	0	0
When you count +1 you are	9	-0.32	0	32
in error 1 % compared	X	-0.90	-1	10 (4)
to the other counts	A	-1.06	-1	6

Average Percent of error each card 18.31 %

	2	3	4	5	6	7	8	9	X	A
53				D	D					
9	D	D	D							
10							D	D		
11									D	D
12		S	S	S	S					
13	S	S	S							
14	S									
15										
16									S	
A2			D	D						
A3			D							
A4		D	D							
A5			D							
A6	D									
A7	D	D								S
A8			D	D	D					
A9										
AA										
22			P	P						
33										
44				D	D					
66	P	P	P							
77									S	
88										
99	P	P								

YOU DO IF THE COUNT IS PLUS ONE
BLANK SPACES ARE BASIC STRATEGY

THESE PLAYS YOU ALWAYS MAKE

2-3-4-5-6 UP   YOU STAND ON 15-16
7-8-9-ACE UP   HIT TIL YOU GET 17
TEN   UP   HIT TIL YOU GET 16

AA,33,77,88   SPLIT AS BASIC

DOUBLE ON 9   ALWAYS 5 OR 6 UP
DOUBLE ON 10   ALWAYS 2 THRU 7 UP
DOUBLE ON 11   ALWAYS 2 THRU 9 UP
DOUBLE A6-A7   ALWAYS 4-5-6   UP

LEARN THIS CHART FIRST

13 2		22 5		13 3		72 6		13 6
44 6		A3 4		A6 3		10 9		11 9
A7 3		16 X		22 3		A8 3		A4 4
63 7		54 3		99 2		A4 3		66 4
A8 6		14 3		12 3		99 3		A8 5
A7 2		A6 2		33 4		44 5		12 4
12 2		63 5		10 7		16 9		11 8
A2 4		66 2		14 2		33 3		63 4
15 X		A2 5		12 6		13 5		99 4
A5 4		63 2		22 4		11 X		10 X
62 6		11 A		88 X		66 5		22 6
14 4		53 4		14 5		14 6		A2 6

WHEN DO YOU DOUBLE ON 10
WHEN DO YOU SPLIT 33
WHEN DO YOU STAND ON 12
WHEN DO YOU HIT A7
WHEN DO YOU DOUBLE ON 8
WHEN DO YOU SPLIT 99
WHEN DO YOU DOUBLE ON A6
WHEN DO YOU HIT 16
WHEN DO YOU STAND ON 77
WHEN DO YOU HIT A8
WHEN DO YOU STAND ON 13
WHEN DO YOU SPLIT 66
WHEN DO YOU DOUBLE ON A7
WHEN DO YOU SPLIT 88
WHEN DO YOU STAND ON A6
WHEN DO YOU DOUBLE ON A4
WHEN DO YOU STAND ON 16
WHEN DO YOU SPLIT 22
WHEN DO YOU DOUBLE ON A2
WHEN DO YOU SPLIT 77
WHEN DO YOU HIT 12
WHEN DO YOU STAND ON 99
WHEN DO YOU SPLIT 44
WHEN DO YOU STAND ON A7
WHEN DO YOU DOUBLE ON 9
WHEN DO YOU DOUBLE ON A8

	2	3	4	5	6	7	8	9	X	A
53				D	D					
9			D	D	D	D				
10	D	D	D	D	D	D				
11	D	D	D	D	D	D	D	D		
12	H	H				H	H	H	H	H
13						H	H	H	H	H
14						H	H	H	H	H
15						H	H	H	H	H
16						H	H	H	H	H
A2			D	D	D					
A3			D	D	D					
A4			D	D	D					
A5			D	D	D					
A6	D	D	D	D	D	H	H	H	H	H
A7		D	D	D	D			H	H	
A8					D					
A9										
22		P	P	P	P	P				
33		P	P	P	P					
44				D	D					
66	P	P	P	P	P					
77	P	P	P	P	P	P			S	
99	P	P	P	P	P		P	P		

ALWAYS SPLIT AA,88

WHEN YOU CAN ANSWER THE
QUESTIONS INSTANTLY YOU
KNOW HOW TO PLAY 21.

	2	3	4	5	6	7	8	9	X	A
53				D	D					
9	D	D	D							
10							D	D		
11									D	D
12		S	S	S	S					
13	S	S	S							
14	S									
15										
16									S	
A2			D	D						
A3			D							
A4		D	D							
A5			D							
A6	D									
A7	D	D								S
A8			D	D	D					
A9										
AA										
22		P	P							
33										
44				D	D					
66	P	P	P							
77								S		
88										
99	P	P								

YOU DO IF THE COUNT IS PLUS ONE

BLANK SPACES ARE BASIC STRATEGY

THESE PLAYS YOU ALWAYS MAKE

2-3-4-5-6 UP   YOU STAND ON 15-16

7-8-9-ACE UP   HIT TIL YOU GET 17

TEN   UP   HIT TIL YOU GET 16

AA,33,77,88   SPLIT AS BASIC

DOUBLE ON 9   ALWAYS 5 OR 6 UP

DOUBLE ON 10   ALWAYS 2 THRU 7 UP

DOUBLE ON 11   ALWAYS 2 THRU 9 UP

DOUBLE A6-A7   ALWAYS 4-5-6   UP

LEARN THIS CHART FIRST

13 2	22 5	13 3	72 6	13 6
44 6	A3 4	A6 3	10 9	11 9
A7 3	16 X	22 3	A8 3	A4 4
63 7	54 3	99 2	A4 3	66 4
A8 6	14 3	12 3	99 3	A8 5
A7 2	A6 2	33 4	44 5	12 4
12 2	63 5	10 7	16 9	11 8
A2 4	66 2	14 2	33 3	63 4
15 X	A2 5	12 6	13 5	99 4
A5 4	63 2	22 4	11 X	10 X
62 6	11 A	88 X	66 5	22 6
14 4	53 4	14 5	14 6	A2 6

WHEN DO YOU DOUBLE ON 10

WHEN DO YOU SPLIT 33

WHEN DO YOU STAND ON 12

WHEN DO YOU HIT A7

WHEN DO YOU DOUBLE ON 8

WHEN DO YOU SPLIT 99

WHEN DO YOU DOUBLE ON A6

WHEN DO YOU HIT 16

WHEN DO YOU STAND ON 77

WHEN DO YOU HIT A8

WHEN DO YOU STAND ON 13

WHEN DO YOU SPLIT 66

WHEN DO YOU DOUBLE ON A7

WHEN DO YOU SPLIT 88

WHEN DO YOU STAND ON A6

WHEN DO YOU DOUBLE ON A4

WHEN DO YOU STAND ON 16

WHEN DO YOU SPLIT 22

WHEN DO YOU DOUBLE ON A2

WHEN DO YOU SPLIT 77

WHEN DO YOU HIT 12

WHEN DO YOU STAND ON 99

WHEN DO YOU SPLIT 44

WHEN DO YOU STAND ON A7

WHEN DO YOU DOUBLE ON 9

WHEN DO YOU DOUBLE ON A8

	2	3	4	5	6	7	8	9	X	A
53				D	D					
9	D	D	D	D						
10	D	D	D	D	D	D	D			
11	D	D	D	D	D	D	D	D	D	D
12	H	H				H	H	H	H	H
13						H	H	H	H	H
14						H	H	H	H	H
15						H	H	H	H	H
16						H	H	H	H	H
A2			D	D	D					
A3			D	D	D					
A4			D	D	D					
A5			D	D	D					
A6	D	D	D	D	D	H	H	H	H	H
A7	D	D	D	D				H	H	
A8					D					
A9										
22		P	P	P	P	P				
33		P	P	P	P					
44				D	D					
66	P	P	P	P	P					
77	P	P	P	P	P	P			S	
99	P	P	P	P	P		P	P		

ALWAYS SPLIT AA,88

WHEN YOU CAN ANSWER THE QUESTIONS INSTANTLY YOU KNOW HOW TO PLAY 21.

Lawrence Revere died early in 1977 of cancer. He was widely acknowledged as the true "master of blackjack" and this book, PLAYING BLACKJACK AS A BUSINESS is one of the largest selling books on the subject.

Twenty-eight of his sixty-one years were devoted to studying the game of blackjack and refining strategies. Revere was constantly utilizing computer technology to make his system the most effective of them all.

Blackjack was his life and it was Revere's wish that his work be continued after his death. This is being done with *Lawrence Revere Ltd.*

NOTES